One More Stripe
to the Tiger

One More Stripe to the Tiger

A Selection of Contemporary
Chilean Poetry and Fiction

Edited and Translated by Sandra Reyes

The University of Arkansas Press
Fayetteville   London   1989

DESIGNER: Chiquita Babb
TYPEFACE: Linotron 202 Galliard
TYPESETTER: G&S Typesetters, Inc.
PRINTER: Edwards Brothers, Inc.
BINDER: Edwards Brothers, Inc.

The paper used in this publication meets the minimum requirements of the
American National Standard for Permanence of Paper for Printed Library
Materials z39.48-1984. ∞

LIBRARY OF CONGRESS CATALOGING-IN-PUBLICATION DATA

One more stripe to the tiger: a selection of contemporary Chilean
    poetry and fiction/edited and translated by Sandra Reyes.
           p.   cm.
      Includes index.
      ISBN 1-55728-034-7 (alk. paper). ISBN 1-55728-035-5 (pbk.: alk. paper)
        1. Chilean literature—20th century—Translations into English.
    2. English literature—20th century—Translations from Spanish.
    I. Reyes, Sandra, 1954–
    PQ8044.O54 1989
    860'.8—dc19   88-20945
                                                                CIP

ONE MORE STRIPE
TO THE TIGER

What does water mean to a fish,
a stripe to the tiger in the eternal book
to the albatross a few more hours of flight?
Camels will pass through needles' eyes
poets through the portals of judgment
the tiger—poem of a thousand lines—
sublime animal—growls underground
swipes at its own shadow
stripes the walls of its tomb in silence.

—*Juan Camerón*

CONTENTS

ACKNOWLEDGMENTS

THE POETRY

Poems by Nicanor Parra were taken from *Hojas de Parra*, Editorial Ganymedes, Santiago.

"Escrito con 'L,'" "Alguien escribe en el viento," "Versículos," and "Herejía" by Gonzalo Rojas were taken from *Oscuro*, by Gonzalo Rojas, Editorial Monte Avilia, Caracas. "Contra la muerte" was taken from *Gonzalo Rojas: 50 poemas*, edited by David Turkeltaub, Editorial Ganymedes, Santiago.

"La caída de un obispo" and "Donde lloran los valientes" by Fernando Alegría were taken from *Changing Centuries*, Latin American Review Press, Pittsburgh.

"Yo sé que en esta lampara apareces" by Miguel Arteche was taken from *Antología de 20 Anos*, Miguel Arteche, Editorial Universitaria, Santiago.

The poem by José Donoso was taken from *Poemas de un novelista*, José Donoso, Editorial Ganymedes, Santiago.

"Nada que ver en la mirada," "Escombro," and "Leones de los novecientos" by Enrique Lihn were taken from *A Partir de Manhattan*, Enrique Lihn, Editorial Ganymedes, Santiago.

"La vida está en la calle" by Delia Domínguez was taken from *El sol mira para atrás*, Delia Domínguez, Editorial Lord Cochrane, Santiago.

"Aquí hay algún error" by Carlos Cortínez was taken from *Treinta y trés*, Carlos Cortínez, Colecciones La Muralla, Madrid.

"Después de todo," "Para hablar con los muertos," and "Lewis Carroll" by Jorge Teillier were taken from *Muertes y maravillas*, Jorge Teillier, Editorial Universitaria, Santiago.

Poems by Armando Uribe Arce were taken from *No hay lugar,* Armando Uribe Arce, Editorial Universitaria, Santiago.

"Informe del tiempo," "De pronto comprendí," "Carta abierta," "La Muerte interrumpe la rutina," and "Como el último bloque" were taken from *Hombrecito verde,* by David Turkeltaub, Editorial Ganymedes, Santiago. "La Poesía sirve para todo" was taken from *Ganymedes 6,* Editorial Ganymedes, Santiago.

"El Centro del dormitorio" by Oscar Hahn was taken from *Ganymedes 6.* "Don Juan" and "Gladiolos junto al mar" were taken from *Arte de Morir,* Oscar Hahn, Ediciones Hispaméricas, Buenos Aires.

Poems by Hernán Lavín Cerda were taken from *Ciegamente los ojos* by Hernán Lavín Cerda, Universidad Nacional Autónoma de Mexico.

"Contra natura," "Sueño," "Que rueda la cabeza del poeta" by Manuel Silva Acevedo were taken from *Mester de bastardía,* Manuel Silva Acevedo, Ediciones El Viento en la Llama, Santiago. "La rata" by Manuel Silva Acevedo was taken from *Ganymedes 6.*

"La ondina" by Naín Nómez, "Correspondencia," "Carcel," "La Pausa" and "El Fusilado" by Gonzalo Millán were taken from *Literatura chilena en Canadá,* edited by Naín Nómez, Ediciones Cordillera, Ottawa.

"Una raya más al tigre" by Juan Camerón and the poems by Armando Rubio and Antonio Vieyra were taken from Diéz Poetas Chilenos (Spanisch-Deutsch) by Enrique Moro, Zambón Verlag, Frankfurt.

"Areas verdes" by Raúl Zurita was taken from *Purgatorio,* Raúl Zurita, Editorial Universitaria, Santiago.

"Familias" by Marjorie Agosín was taken from *Hogueras,* Marjorie Agosín, Editorial Universitaria, Santiago.

THE FICTION

"The Missionary" first appeared as "El misionero" by Enrique Campos Menéndez, in *Cuentos chilenos contemporáneas,* Editorial Andrés Bello, Santiago.

"The Unmarriage" was published as "Incommunicación" by Cecilia Casanova, in the book *Paraguas,* by Cecilia Casanova, Santiago.

"Santelices" was published as "Santelices" by José Donoso, in *Antología del cuento chileno,* Enrique La Fourcade, Editorial Importadora Alfa, Santiago.

"Duo" was published as "Dúo" by Luis Domínguez, in *Citroneta blues,* Luis Domínguez, Editorial Universitaria, Santiago.

"Damelza" was published as "Damelza de Greenwich Village" by José Luís Rosasco in *Hoy día es mañana,* José Luís Rosasco, Santiago.

"But Life" was published as "Pero la vida" by Poli Délano, in *25 Años y algo más,* Poli Délano, Alfa Contemporánea, Santiago.

"Sweet Companion" was published as "Dulce companía" by Marta Blanco in *Antología del cuento chileno,* Enrique La Fourcade, Editorial Importadora Alfa, Santiago.

"Law of Escape" was published as "Ley de fuga" by Carlos Pastén in *Literatura chilena en Canadá,* Ediciones Cordillera, Ottawa.

"The Earth-Eater" was published as "El comedor de tierras" by Juan Carlos García in *Araucaria no. 12,* Ediciones Michay, Madrid.

"The Flood" was published as "Inundación" by Juan Carlos García, in *Literatura chilena en Canadá.*

"A Drop of Immortality" was published as "Una Gota de inmortalidad" by Carlos Iturra in *El Cuento chileno contemporáneo,* Editorial Andrés Bello, Santiago.

Special thanks to José Luís Rosasco, David Turkeltaub, and Delia Domínguez for their assistance. Many thanks to all the publishers for granting permissions that made this book possible, but especially to Editorial Ganymedes and Editorial Universitaria for their great assistance.

Finally, I would like to thank Larry Perry at the University of Arkansas Library and all the library staff who assisted in author searches and helped locate books of Chilean literature.

One More Stripe to the Tiger

INTRODUCTION

NEW CHILEAN WRITING

FROM the beginning of the Modernist movement, manifested in the works of Rubén Darío, through the generation of Sólar, Mouré, Veléz, and Huidobro to the present-day influences of Pablo Neruda and Nicanor Parra, the poetry of Chile has undergone a series of evolutionary changes. It bears the strong markings of an art which is decidedly Chilean, yet still universal in its appeal.

Traditionally, before Neruda and for some time after, Chilean poetry was formally rigid in structure; it was, as was most American and European poetry, hanging on to older forms and stylistics while at the same time conscientiously striving to grasp the new. The past three decades, however, reveal the emergence of remarkably distinct poetic themes and trends. It is obvious that the Chilean poets of this generation mean to produce, not a narrow national poetry, but a human poetry that is direct, forceful, devoid of ostentation and unnecessary decor, and which presents old themes in fresh ways.

A number of poets of the eighties, both older and younger, seem to be striving toward a common goal: the mastery of a poetry which, though brief, is not epigrammatic, not "easy," yet clearly executed. The best of these contemporary poets show superb technical control, often producing a poetic cadence which is strong yet so subtle it is not perceived at first reading.

Free verse and the prose poem are popular, but many poets, like Enrique Lihn and Oscar Hahn, are equally comfortable writing sonnets and other structured forms including hendecasyllabic verse, both rhymed and unrhymed. At the same time, some writers are seeking to liberate themselves from conventional modes of expression by substituting repetition, anaphora, and heavy enjambment for traditional rhyme and meter, creating tones of bland cynicism, suppressing the intensity of passion which flows throughout their work. Sometimes a light sentimentality is created—nostalgic, but not overly lyrical. Some experimentalists deal heavily with the abstract, using collage poetry, physical poetry, or any poetic innovation as a means of making a statement and breaking with tradition. Their attempts are admirable; the effects are varied, exciting, and challenging to both the critic and the poet.

Chilean fiction, like most fiction of this generation, is highly variant. It runs the spectrum from traditional to abstract/experimental with some surrealistic and metaphysical trends falling somewhere in between. Common themes include the search for love, the search for individualism, nostalgia for the past, and contemporary social problems. The styles and types of Chilean fiction today are as numerous as the writers themselves. This richness of subject and diversity of style, together with a gentle irony, is much of what makes Chilean fiction, as well as the poetry, such a pleasure to read. The many manifestations of these elements, more as attitude than technique, account for the great differences among the works included here.

In compiling and translating this collection, I faced two equally demanding challenges. The first was the selection process itself. It was, of course, impossible to represent all good Chilean writers past and present. It was not even possible to represent all good Chilean writers of the past three decades. The object here, then, is not so much to show an English version of every good poem and story written in Chile in the past twenty years, but rather to present a cross-section of the writing that has been taking shape there since the late sixties. My goal was to achieve a healthy balance between representative works of some well-known authors and those of some newer writers whose works show signs of becoming a part of Chile's literary heritage.

The second challenge, especially in regard to the fiction, was that of dealing with the works of many individual authors with clearly distinct styles, and then dealing with the individuality of each piece without allowing it to become a stereotypical sample of that author's work. These translations attempt to maintain an acute sensitivity to the uniqueness of style and tone of each poem and story, while at the same time letting the author's voice be heard as it was heard in Spanish, inasmuch as this is possible. This objective has governed diction, semantics, and idiom and has dominated every choice of rhetorical peculiarity as far as those peculiarities can be carried. (How many ways can one say, "He removed a watch from his pocket."?) I aimed at avoiding the intrusion of the translator's voice, for each piece has its own personality, a unique quality that I tried to capture while keeping within the limitations of the original. These challenges, though difficult, when successfully met are the delights of the translation process. They are what makes it work, and they are fun.

S. R.

The Poetry

Nicanor Parra

was born in 1914 in Chillán, a small town in the south of Chile. His first book of poems, *Cancionero sin Nombre,* was awarded the *Premio Municipal de Poesía* the following year. *Poemas y Anti-poemas* won two awards, the *Premio del Sindicato de Escritores* and the *Premio Municipal.* Among his many works are *Obra Gruesa, Versos del Salón, Canciones Rusas,* and *Discursos* (a critical work co-authored with Pablo Neruda). More recent works include *Sermones y Predicas del Cristo de Elqui, Nuevos Sermones y Predicas,* and *Hojas de Parra (Ganymedes).* He lives in Santiago, Chile, where he is Professor of Theoretical Physics at the University of Santiago.

NOTA SOBRE
LA LECCION DE LA ANTIPOESIA

1. En la antipoesía se busca la poesía, no la elocuencia.
2. Los antipoemas deben leerse en el mismo órden en que fueron escritos.
3. Hemos de leer con el mismo gusto los poemas que los antipoemas.
4. La poesía pasa—la antipoesía también.
5. El poeta nos habla a todos
   sin hacer diferencia de nada.
6. Nuestra curiosidad nos impide muchas veces gozar plenamente la antipoesía por tratar de entender y discutir aquello que no se debe.
7. Si quieres aprovechar, lee de buena fe y no te complazcas jamás en el nombre del literato.
8. Pregunta con buena voluntad y oye sin replicar la palabra de los poetas: no te disgusten las sentencias de los viejos pues no las profieren al acaso.
9. Saludos a todos.

A NOTE ABOUT
THE READING OF ANTIPOETRY

1. In antipoetry you look for poetry ineloquence.
2. Antipoems should be read in the same order they were written.
3. Read poetry with the same depth of pleasure as antipoetry.
4. Poetry passes—antipoetry also.
5. The poet speaks to all of us
   making no distinction.
6. Our curiosity is often a hindrance to our full pleasure of
   antipoetry by causing us to try to understand and argue
   something we should not.
7. If you want to truly enjoy, read in good faith and not because of
   the writer's name.
8. Ask in good will and listen to the poet without contradicting.
   Don't scorn the logic of the old ones.
9. Best regards.

CAMBIOS

Cambio lola de 30
x 2 viejas de 15

Cambio torta de novia
x un par de muletas eléctricas

Cambio gato enfermo de meningitis
x aguafuerte del siglo XVIII

Cambio volcán en erupción permanente
x helecóptero poco uso

Cambio gato x liebre

Cambio zapato izquierdo x derecho.

TRADING

Trade you a thirty-year-old foxy lady
for two fifteen-year-old senile women

Trade you a wedding cake
for a pair of electric crutches

Trade you a cat sick with meningitis
for an eighteenth-century brandy

Trade you a volcano in permanent eruption
for a helicopter like new

Trade you a cat for a jackrabbit

Trade you a left shoe for a right shoe.

DESVALIJEMOS A ESTE VIEJO VERDE

tú le sacas el lápiz
mientras yo le sustraigo la corbata
no le dejemos piedra sobre piedra
yo le extraigo los dientes amarillos
sácale tú los calcetines de lana

y comenzaron a robarle toda la plata

le robaron un litro de bencina
dos o tres metros de papel higiénico
cuatro sobres aéreos
toda su biblioteca pornográfica
siete manzanas—ocho huevos duros
media docena de claveles rojos
nueve cajas de fósforos
y una barbaridad de alfileres de gancho

hasta que el viejo pillo despertó
y las hizo ponerse en cuatro patas

LET'S LOOT THIS DIRTY OLD MAN

you get his pencils
I'll take the tie
let's not leave one stone unturned
I'll take his yellow dentures
you get those wool socks

next they start taking his money

they take a quart of kerosene
two or three rolls of toilet paper
four air mail envelopes
his pornographic library
seven apples—eight boiled eggs
half a dozen red carnations
nine boxes of matches
and a humongous horde of safety pins

till suddenly the old geezer comes back to life
and knocks them all back on their haunches

EL PREMIO NOBEL

El Premio Nóbel de Lectura
me lo debieran dar a mí
que soy el lector ideal
y leo todo lo que pillo:

Leo los nombres de las calles
y los letreros luminosos
y las murallas de los baños
y las nuevas listas de precios

y las noticias policiales
y los pronósticos del Derby

y las patentes de los autos

para un sujeto como yo
la palabra es algo sagrado

señores miembros del jurado
qué ganaría con mentirles
soy un lector empedernido

me leo todo—no me salto
ni los avisos económicos

claro que ahora leo poco
no dispongo de mucho tiempo
pero caramba que he leído

THE NOBEL PRIZE

The Nobel Prize in Reading
should be awarded to me
since I am the ideal reader
I read everything I see written:

I read street names
neon signs
bathroom graffiti
new price tags

police notices
Derby predictions

automobile license plates

for somebody like me
the written word's a sacred thing

ladies and gentlemen of the panel
there's no use lying about it
I'm a hard-boiled reader

I read everything—
even reports on the economy

of course these days I don't read as much as I used to
I don't have a lot of time on my hands
but hell the stuff I've read in my lifetime

por eso pido que me den
el Premio Nóbel de Lectura
a la brevedad imposible

VIOLACION

Un sillón acusado
de faltarle el respeto a una silla
alegó que la silla
había sido la culpable de todo
se desnudó por propia iniciativa
mientras yo conversaba por teléfono
qué quería que hiciera señor juez
pero la silla dijo violación
y el acusado fue declarado culpable

so I urgently implore you to bestow upon me
the Nobel Prize in Reading
at your earliest impossible convenience

RAPE

A cushion accused
of violating a chair
advocated that the chair
had been totally at fault
it had disrobed itself of its own free will
while I was talking on the telephone
what was I to do Your Honor
but the chair screamed rape
and the accused was pronounced guilty

QUE GANA UN VIEJO
CON HACER GIMNASIA

Qué ganará con hablar por teléfono
qué ganará con hacerse famoso
qué gana un viejo con mirarse al espejo

Nada
hundirse cada vez más en el fango

Ya son las tres o cuatro de la madrugada
por qué no trata de quedarse dormido
pero no—déle con hacer gimnasia
déle con los llamaditos de larga distancia
déle con Bach
          con Beethoven
               con Tchaikovsky
déle con las miradas al espejo
déle con la obsesión de seguir respirando

lamentable—mejor apagara la luz

Viejo ridículo le dice su madre
eres exactamente igual a tu padre
él tampoco quería morir
Dios te dé vida para andar en auto
Dios te dé vida para hablar por teléfono
Dios te dé vida para respirar
Dios te dé vida para enterrar a tu madre

¡Te quedaste dormido viejo ridículo!
pero el anciano no piensa dormir
no confundir llorar con dormir

WHAT GOOD IS IT FOR
AN OLD MAN TO WORK OUT IN THE GYM

What good is it to talk on the phone
what good is being famous
what good is it for an old man to look in the mirror

No good
he just sinks deeper into the muck

It must be three or four o'clock in the morning
why doesn't he try to get some sleep
but no—leave him to his work-outs in the gym
leave him to his long distance phone calls
leave him to his Bach
                    his Beethoven
                              his Tchaikovsky
leave him to his primping in front of the mirror
leave him to his obsession to go on breathing

how pathetic—why doesn't he just turn out the light

Old fool his mother tells him
you're just like your father
he didn't want to die either
God grant you strength to drive your car
God grant you strength to talk on the phone
God grant you strength to keep breathing
God grant you strength to bury your mother

You're asleep old fool!
but the old man wouldn't dream of sleeping
not to confuse weeping with sleeping

EL VERDADERO PROBLEMA
de la Filosofía

es quién lava los platos
nada del otro mundo
Dios
        la verdad
                    el transcurso del tiempo
claro que sí
pero primero quién lava los platos

el que quiera lavarlos que los lave
chao pescao
                    y tan enemigos como antes

THE GREAT ENIGMA
of Philosophy

is who's going to wash the dishes
it isn't life after death
God
      truth
             the passage of time
these things are important
but first who's going to wash the dishes

he who wants to wash them let him wash them
see you later alligator
                      and true enemies forever

POESIA POESIA todo poesía

hacemos poesía
hasta cuando vamos a la sala de baño

palabras textuales del Cristo de Elqui

mear es hacer poesía
tan poesía como tañer el laúd
o cagar o poetizar o tirarse peos

y vamos viendo qué es la poesía

palabras textuales del Profeta de Elqui

POETRY POETRY all is poetry

we write poetry
even when we go to the bathroom

scriptural words of the Christ of Elqui

pissing is poetry
it's as much poetry as strumming a lute
or farting or poeticizing or taking a crap

and now we see what poetry really is

scriptural words of the Prophet of Elqui

DEBAJO DE MI CAMA

tengo enterrada a mi esposa legítima

la maté en un rapto de ira
hace una porrada de años

a medianoche despierto sobresaltado
tengo frío señora
por qué no sube a calentarme los huesos

ella jamás se hace de rogar
por el contrario sube motu prop(r)io
cuando yo no la llamo puntualmente

y se abalanza sobre mi cadáver
y me despierta a abrazos y besos
y parecemos un trigal en llamas

UNDER MY BED

I have my legal wife buried

I killed her in a fit of rage
a few years back

at midnight I wake up topsy-turvy
I'm cold, woman
why don't you come up and warm my cold bones

she never makes a man beg
in fact she comes up of her own free will
whenever I don't call her punctually

and she throws herself on my cadaver
and she wakes me with hugs and kisses
and we're like a wheat field on fire

Gonzalo Rojas

was born in Lebu, Chile, in 1917. His poetry has been published in Chile, Venezuela, Spain, and Mexico. His work has been translated into English and other languages. Among his highly praised poetical works are: *La Misería del hombre, Contra La muerte, Oscuro, Transtierro,* and *Del Relámpago*. A collection of his selected poetry has been compiled into a book entitled *Gonzalo Rojas: 50 Poemas,* by Ganymedes. Rojas presently resides in Santiago.

VERSICULOS

A esto vino al mundo el hombre, a combatir
la serpiente que avanza en el silbido
de las cosas, entre el fulgor
y el frenesí, como un polvo centellante, a besar
por dentro el hueso de la locura, a poner
amor y más amor en la sábana
del huracán, a escribir en la cópula
el relámpago de seguir siendo, a jugar
este juego de respirar en el peligro.

A esto vino al mundo el hombre, a esto la mujer
de su costilla: a usar este traje con usura,
esta piel de lujuría, a comer este fulgor de fragrancia
cortos dias que caben adentro de unas decadas
en la nebulosa de los milenios, a ponerse
a cada instante la máscara, a inscribirse en el número de los justos
de acuerdo con las leyes de la historia o del arca
de la salvación: a esto vino el hombre.

Hasta que es cortado y arrojado a esto vino, hasta que lo desovan
como a un pescado con el cuchillo, hasta
que el desnacido sin estallar regresa a su átomo,
con la humildad de la piedra,
                              cae entonces,
sigue cayendo nueve meses, sube
ahora de golpe, pasa desde la oruga
de la vejez a otra mariposa
distinta.

IT IS WRITTEN

For this man came into the world, to battle
the serpent advancing toward him in the hissing
of the universe between the brilliance
and the frenzy, like glittering dust, to kiss
the bone of madness from within, to cast
love and more love into the sheets
of the hurricane, to write, in the coupling,
the lightning of continued being, to play
this game of breathing danger.

For this man came into the world, for this woman
taken from his rib: to rent these clothes,
this skin of lust, to eat this brilliant fragrance
the short days that fit inside these decades,
in the nebula of the millennia, constantly
donning the mask, inscribing their names among the members of the
    righteous
in accordance with the laws of history or the arc
of salvation: for this man came.

Until he is cut down and burned for this he came, until they gut him
with a knife, like a fish
until the unborn without bursting out returns to its atom
with the humility of a stone,
                            falling then,
continuing to fall nine months, suddenly
rising, changing from the worm of old age
into the butterfly,
a different butterfly.

HEREJIA

Según el manifesto de las estrellas y esto no es cosa de hoy
ni de ayer, pase lo que pase hay que salvar al hombre
de tanta injusticia, hacerlo grande sin
Inquisición, en un asalto al cielo
libre, pero el pobre
hombre nace y muere solo
con su soledad y su demencia
natural en el bosque
donde no cabe la piedad ni el hacha.

CONTRA LA MUERTE

Me arranco las visiones y me arranco los ojos cada día que pasa.

¡No quiero ver no puedo! ver morir a los hombres cada dia.
Prefiero ser de piedra, estar oscuro,
a soportar el asco de ablandarme por dentro y sonreir
a diestra y a siniestra con tal de prosperar en mi negocio.

HERESY

According to the commandment of the stars and this is not a
    question
of today or yesterday, whatever happens to happen we have to save
    man
from all the injustice, bring him to greatness without
Inquisition, attacking the open sky
but miserable man
is born and dies alone
with loneliness and natural lunacy
in the forest
where there is no place for pity or for the axe.

IN OPPOSITION TO DEATH

I scratch out images and I scratch out my eyes every day that goes by.

I don't want to see I can't! see people dying every day.
I'd rather be made of stone, of dark stone,
than to endure this nauseous melting inside
and this smiling right and left at my prospering business.

No tengo otro negocio que estar aquí diciendo la verdad
en mitad de la calle y hacia todos los vientos:
la verdad de estar vivo, únicamente vivo,
con los pies en la tierra y el esquéleto libre en este mundo.

¿Que sacamos con eso de saltar hasta el sol con nuestras máquinas
a la velocidad del pensamiento, demonios; que sacamos
con volar mas allá del infinito
si seguimos muriendo sin esperanza alguna de vivir
fuera del tiempo oscuro?

Dios no me sirve. Nada me sirve de nada.
Pero respiro, y como, y hasta duermo
pensando que me faltan unos diez o veinte años para irme
de bruces, como todos, a dormir en dos metros de cemento allá
    abajo.

No lloro, no me lloro. Todo ha de ser como ha de ser,
pero no puedo ver cajones y cajones
pasar, pasar, pasar, pasar cada minuto
llenos de algo, rellenos de algo no puedo ver
todavía caliente la sangre en los cajones.

Toco esta rosa, beso sus petales, adoro
la vida, no me canso de amar a las mujeres: me alimento
de abrir el mundo en ellas. Pero todo es inútil.

Porque yo mismo soy una cabeza inútil
lista para cortar, por no entender que es eso
de esperar otro mundo de este mundo.

Me hablan de Dios o me hablan de la Historia. Me río
de ir a buscar tan lejos la explicación del hambre
que me devora, el hambre de vivir como el sol
en la gracia del aire, eternamente.

I have no business except to be here telling the truth
in the middle of the street and telling it to the four winds:
the truth of being alive, singly alive,
with my feet on the ground and my skeleton free in the world.

What's the use of jumping at the sun with our machines
at the speed of thought; damn it all to hell, what's the use
of flying farther and farther into infinity
if we have to keep dying with no hope of living
outside of dark time?

God is no help to me. Nobody is any help to me for anything.
I just keep breathing and eating until I fall asleep
thinking I've got about ten or twenty years left
before I go headlong, like all the rest, to sleep six feet down under a
    cement slab.

I'm not crying; I'm not crying for myself. What has to be
has to be, but I just can't see boxes and boxes
passing, passing, passing, passing by every minute
filled with things, filled up with things, I can't see
the blood still warm in those boxes.

I touch this rose, I kiss its petals, I adore life,
I'm never tired of making love to women—
opening worlds in them is my life's breath. But it's useless.

Because I'm just a useless head
ready to be cut off, for not understanding what it's all about,
for hoping for another world in this world.

They speak to me of God and they speak to me of History.
I scoff at myself for going so far to look for an explanation
of this hunger that devours me, this hunger to live,
forever, like the sun, at the mercy of the air.

UNO ESCRIBE EN EL VIENTO

Que por qué, que hasta cuándo, que si voy a dormir noventa meses,
que moriré sin obra, que el mar se habrá perdido.
Pero yo soy el mar, y no me llamo arruga
ni volumen de nada.

Crezco y crezco en el árbol que va a volar. No hay libro
para escribir el sol. ¿Y la sangre? Trabajo
será que me encuadernen el animal. Poeta
de un tiro: justiciero.

Me acuerdo, tú te acuerdas, todos nos acordamos
de la galaxia ciega desde donde vinimos
con esta luz tan pobre a ver el mundo.
Vinimos, y eso es todo.

Tanto para eso, madre, pero entramos llorando,
pero entramos llorando al laberinto
como si nos cortaran el origen. Después
el carácter, la guerra.

El ojo no podría ver el sol
si él mismo no lo fuera. Cosmonautas, avisen
si es verdad esa estrella, o es también escritura
de la farsa.

Uno escribe en el viento: ¿para qué las palabras?
Arbol, árbol oscuro. El mar arroja lejos
a los pescados muertos. Que lean a los otros.
A mí con mis raíces.

SOMEONE IS WRITING ON THE WIND

That the why, that the until when, that if I should sleep ninety
    months,
that I will die without works, that the sea will be lost.
But I am the sea, and I don't call myself wrinkle
or volume or anything.

I grow and grow into a flying tree. There is no book
to write the sun. And blood? There'll be a work
they can print and bind the animal me into. Poet:
a fair shot.

I remember, you remember, we all remember
the blind galaxy where we came from
and this poor weak light to see the world with.
We came, that's all.

So much for that, Mama, but we came in crying,
we came in crying, to that labyrinth
as if they'd cut off our roots. Then
character, war.

The eye wouldn't see the sun
if there were no sun. Cosmonauts, tell us
if that star is true, or is it false
scripture as well.

Someone is writing on the wind: what are words for?
Tree, dark tree. The sea spews forth
its dead fish. Let them read the others.
Leave me to my roots.

Con mi pueblo de pobres. Me imagino a mi padre
colgado de mis pies y a mi abuelo colgado
de los pies de mi padre. Porque el minero es uno,
y además venceremos.

Venceremos. El mundo se hace con sangre. Iremos
con las tablas al hombro, y el fusil. Una casa
para América hermosa. Una casa, una casa.
Todos somos obreros.

América es la casa: ¿dónde la nebulosa?
Me doy vueltas y vueltas en mi viejo individuo
para nacer. Ni estrella ni madre que me alumbre
lúgubremente solo.

Mortal, mortuorio río. Pasa y pasa el color,
sangra y sangra mi pueblo, corre y corre el sentido.
Pero el dinero pudre con su peste las aguas.
Cambiar, cambiar el mundo.

O dormir en el átomo que hará saltar el aire en cien mil víboras
cráter de las ciudades bellamente viciosas.
Cementerio volante: ¿dónde la realidad?
Hubo una vez un niño.

Leave me my village of poor. I imagine my father
hanging from my feet and my grandfather hanging
from the feet of my father. It is all one,
and still we will conquer.

We will conquer. The world is made of blood. We'll go
with slabs on our shoulders, and muskets. A house
for beautiful America. A house, a house.
We're all builders.

America is the house: where is the fog?
I turn and turn within my old self
to be born. No star, no mother to deliver me
mournfully alone.

Mortal, mortuary river. Color passes and passes,
my people bleed and bleed, the senses flow and flow.
Money pollutes the waters with its plague
To keep the world changing, changing

Or sleeping in the atom that will burst the air into thousands of
      vipers
a crater of cities resplendently overflowing.
Flying cemetery: where's the reality?
Once there was a child.

ESCRITO CON L

Mucha lectura envejece la imaginación
del ojo, suelta todas las abejas pero mata el zumbido
de lo invisible, corre, crece
tentacular, se arrastra, sube al vacío
del vacío, en nombre
del conocimiento, pulpo
de tinta, paraliza la figura del sol
que hay en nosotros, nos
viciosamente mancha.

Mucha lectura entristece, mucha envilece
                              apestamos
a viejos, los griegos
eran los jóvenes, somos nosotros los turbios
como si los papiros dijeran algo distinto al ángel del aire:
somos nosotros los soberbios, ellos eran inocentes,
nosotros los del mosquero, ellos eran los sabios.

Mucha lectura envejece la imaginación
del ojo, suelta todas las abejas pero mata el zumbido
de lo invisible, acaba
no tanto con la L de la famosa lucidez
sino con esa otra L
de la libertad,
de la locura
que ilumina lo hondo
de lo lúgubre

WRITTEN WITH L

Too much reading withers the imagination
of the eye, releases the bees but kills the buzz
of the invisible, runs, grows, with tentacles, rips loose
rises to the heights of the void of emptiness, in the name
of wisdom, the squid
its ink paralyzing the figure of the sun
in all of us, thickly
staining us.

Too much learning saddens, sullies us,

                         we rot

into old age, the Greeks
were the young, we are the turbulent
as if our papyrus had said something different to the angel of air:
we are the passionate and proud, they were innocent,
we are caught in the trap, they were wise.

Too much reading withers the imagination
of the eye, releases the bees but kills the buzz
of the invisible, finishing
not so much with the well-known L of lucidity
but with those other Ls
of liberty
of lunacy
illuminating the depths
of the lugubrious

del laberinto,
          lambda
               loca
                    luciérnaga
antes del fósforo, mucho antes
del latido
del Logos.

a Juan Liscano

the labyrinth,
                lambda
                        ludicrous
                                lightningbug
long before fire, long before
the live beat
of the Logos.

to Juan Liscano

Fernando Alegría

was born in Santiago in 1918. He has been a professor of Spanish and Philosophy at the University of Chile, Doctor of Literature at the University of Columbia, New York, and has served as a professor of Spanish literature at Berkeley and Stanford. He has been a collaborator on numerous literary journals, a critic and essayist, author of several novels and short stories, and has earned numerous literary awards, including the *Premio Municipal de Novela*, the *Premio de la Union Panamericana*, and the *Premio Atenea*. His works have appeared in many anthologies.

DONDE LLORAN LOS VALIENTES

Rodeado de animales
sonriendo
sentado a la diestra del Padre
considerando lo tristeza de acuario que reina en este mundo,
oídme bien:
Otra botella para el campañero que remece la tarde.

¡Pasan tantos peces por el vino,
tantas suaves estrellas que olvidaron
tanto pulpo soplando terciopelo
botando sus lunares en estos tristes bares!

Es porque usted llora en su mesa
y los hombres no lloran, compañero.

Es porque bebo directamente de su costado
y a usted le duele que se apague el mundo
se cubran de cielo estos mármoles
y caigan como dados los últimos garzones.

Nos observa alguien que desciende de una lámpara.

Es preciso que el sol agite sus plumas en el vino
y veamos en silencio el historial de nuestra casa.

Sabe a soledad.

¿Por qué se van los señores de capa y bastón por una alameda en
    llamas?
Arrastran el poncho, es cierto, ordeñan las parras
aúllan siguiendo la humareda del Angelus.

WHERE BRAVE MEN WEEP

Surrounded by animals
smiling
seated at the Father's right hand
contemplating the aquarium sadness that rules this world,
hear me well:
Another bottle for the bellman who tolls the evening.

So many fish pass through this wine,
so many gentle starfish that have forgotten
so many squid blowing out their velvet
throwing off their warts in these sad bars!

That's why you're crying on your table
and men don't cry, my friend.

That's why I'm drinking here beside you
and it's hurting you that the world is going out
that the sky is covering these slabs of marble
and the last waiters are falling out like tossed dice.

Someone's come down from a chandelier and is looking at us.

It's only right that the sun should beat its wings in the wine
and that we in silence should watch the history of our houses.

It tastes like loneliness.

Why are those men going off in top-hats and canes down a flaming
    alley?
I'm sure they're wearing overcoats, they're picking the vines,
they're howling, chasing the incense smoke of the Hail Marys.

Usted lo dice de rodillas, con el oído pegado al suelo.
Pero ¿no siente las violetas, los pájaros, la lluvia en el parrón
todo como volándonos en la garganta?

Es porque usted me bebe directamente del costado
y me duele y nos duele.

Levántese de esas tablas mojadas.
¿No ve que molesta a la dulce familia?
Los niños observan turbados el sagrado corazón que empieza a
    gotearle en el chaleco.
Por este mundo que ahora está quemándonos.
Beba su vino.
Beba tranquilamente los terrores del verrano.
Y cállese.

La vida también aprovecha sus descuidos.

Por ejemplo,
cae una mesa.

La niña vende ojos de cristal en una caja de zapatos.
La muerte borra calladamente sus manchas.
Crece el vino de los barrios.
De pronto estamos todos como buenos hermanos
alrededor de una bella ciudad en primavera.

Los almacenes se cargan de frutos amarillos
y es el Padre quien nos llama sentado en su silla de paja.
¿No oye usted el jubilado cantando como un triste gallo en la
    alborada?
Dejemos que golpee ese extraño alguacil su penitencia en los platos.
Pide salvación pero no se decide el maldito.
¿No le ha visto entrar varias veces,
de a poco,
provocando, fresco y sabio como un cristal que se burla,
como una hiena insegura, como un inspector de penas

You say yours on your knees, your ear glued to the ground.
But can't you hear the violets, the birds, the rain on the grape
feel it all fluttering in our throats?

That's why you're drinking here beside me
and it's hurting me and hurting us.

Get up off the wet floor.
Can't you see you're disturbing that nice family?
The children are getting nervous watching the sacred heart
    beginning to drip from your jacket.
For this world is already starting to burn us.
Drink your wine.
Drink calmly the terrors of the summer.
And be quiet.

Life also profits from its mistakes.

For example,
a table falls.

A little girl is selling glass eyes from a shoebox.
Death is quietly erasing its stains.
The wine of the community is growing.
All of a sudden we're all good brothers
in some beautiful city in springtime.

The stores are stocked with yellow fruit
and it's the Father who's calling us from his wicker chair.
Can't you hear the senior citizen crowing like a sad rooster at dawn?
Let that strange patrolman beat out his penitence on the dishes.
He asks for salvation, but the bastard can't make up his mind.
Haven't you seen him in here before,
sneaking in,
stirring up trouble, tricky as a fun-house mirror,
acting like a shy hyena, like a pain inspector,

indeciso, sin pestañas, pasando de una mano a otra, eternamente,
el tinto y el blanco?
¿Qué quiere? ¿A dónde va? ¿De donde viene?
¿Por qué entra cada cierto tiempo a beber su sangre y la mía?
¿A qué barra pertenece?
¿A la selección morada de insomnes
vampiros moribundos que toman fotos en el parque?
Me da una rabia.
¡Y, sin embargo, la vida!

No se caiga de la silla, compañero.

El piano recibe la lluvia como un balde.

Puede ser que ahí este la razón de tanto olvido.
Y tanta angustia.
Así, pues, la noche blanca, las últimas estrellas.
la esperma que deja sus flores de sangre entre las sabanas.

No he pedido nada.

¿Por qué llama?
Quisiéramos vivir de nuevo.
¿Es todo lo que se ofrece?
Acaso he pedido una antigua amiga,
ésa que daba su aliento a los helechos del río
la que salía de azules cartulinas quitándose los guantes,
no era sino un vestido soplado por lentas caracolas
unas hojas de música
octubre o diciembre.

Ha pasado rodando un cartero.

La conciencia es un saco de arena
saber que se ha perdido la familia
que me ven que no me ven que los veo
y se han sacado la boca y me la entregan.

wishy-washy, no eyelashes, always changing
the red wine and the white wine
from one hand to the other?
What does he want? Where's he going? Where's he coming from?
Why does he always come here to drink your blood and mine?
What party does he belong to?
To that purple group of sleepwalkers,
dying vampires taking pictures in the park?
It makes me furious.
But anyway, that's life!

Try not to fall off the chair, friend.

The piano is catching the rain like a bucket.

That could be the reason there's so much forgetting.
And so much anguish.
And that could explain the reason for the white night, the last stars,
the sperm that leaves its bloody flowers between the sheets.

I haven't asked for anything.

Why are you calling?
We would like to try living again.
Is that all you want?
Perhaps I might ask for an old girlfriend,
the one who breathed on the ferns by the river,
the one who would come out of blue cardboard taking off her gloves;
she was only a dress blown by slow snails
some sheets of music
October or December.

A mailman just rolled by.

Conscience is a bag of sand
to know that the family is lost
let them see me not see me not see them
and they've taken off their mouths and given them to me.

Usted no escucha.
¿Quién escucha ya?
A esta hora, a los sesenta y tantos de edad,
tendido en una ambulancia gris.
Mirándome
pasa algo que se parece a mí.

Déje florecer ese jarro.
No lo toque.
El borgoña es un árbol de verano.
Que salgan los dedos del vino
la garganta morada de la vida
y el vino comience a crear el mundo otra vez.

Debo salir.

Dios no tiene tiempo de esconderse.

Volveré con otros animales
desplomando el domingo sobre la cordillera rosada
preguntando
por qué somos una pelota dorada como usted dice.

Debo salir.
No me para nadie.

Piense en el pastor que se fue por un laberinto de lagares
así, estrellándose en la noche
destapando corchos con la boca
arrancándose viejos hongos del pecho.
Oiga.
Un viento airado azota el urinario
agua de la edad de oro resbalando como una mano el mármol.

En su silla de paja el púgil pasa las toallas
agradecido de la vida
tirando la cadena.
¡Cómo se defiende ese hombre del chal rojo!

You are not listening.
Who listens anymore?
At this hour, at sixty some-odd years,
stretched out in a gray ambulance.
Staring at me.
It's passing by and it looks like me.

Let that jug bloom.
Don't touch it.
Burgundy is a summer tree.
Let the fingers come out of the wine
the purple throat of life
and the wine starts creating the world again.

I have to go.

God has no time to hide.

I'll come back with other animals
collapsing the Sundays on the pink cordillera
asking
why we're a gold-plated ball as you say.

I have to go.
Don't anyone try to stop me.

Think of the shepherd who went off into a labyrinth of winepresses
just like that, exploding into the night
popping corks with his teeth
digging old mushrooms from his chest.
Listen.
A furious wind is whipping through the urinal
water from the Golden Age gliding like a hand over the marble.

From his wicker chair the boxer hands out towels
contented with life
flushing the toilet.
See how the one in the red fights back!

Tiene pegadas en la cara algunas cosas
su memoria y la mía.

Dios espera dándole cuerda a su reloj
y el triste ciruelo deja caer sus ampolletas.

Se ha degollado un lustrabotas.
¿Para qué?
Así es que el hombre no es más que una manga de paño
una cabeza de vino tinto
un sordo rocío
algo triste, pero algo de repente
pensando.
Y se fue otra vez la vida y otra vez vuelve en un vaso.

Beber es saber.

¿Quién eres?
El hombre repetido algunas veces
perdiendo terreno, morado y palpitante
sujetándose el cielo con las manos

Prefiero inclinarme y beberte
no reparar en tu violencia
dudar de tu sombra en la pared
borrar con un gesto final a los extraños.

Ya están cerrando el mundo.

El vino es un ángel chorreado batiendo alas.

Parroquianos de esta vida que va aclarando
¡A volar por el tragaluz!

He has some things sticking to his face
his memory and mine.

God winds his watch waiting
and the sad plum tree drops its hourglasses.

A shoeshiner has cut his head off.
What for?
So then a man is no more than a sleeve to wipe his nose on
a head of red wine
a dull drizzle
a sad thing but something suddenly
thinking.
And life gets away again and again comes back in a glass.
Drinking is knowing.

Who are you?
Man repeated over and over
losing ground, purple and palpitating
holding up the heavens with his hands

I'd rather lean forward and drink you
than to defend your violence
doubt your shadow on the wall
erase all the strangeness with a wave of my hands.

Now they're closing up the world.

The wine is a dripping angel flapping its wings.

Customers in a world getting clearer and clearer.
Up and out through the skylight!

LA CAIDA DE UN OBISPO

Que repiquen las campanas
el obispo viene volando
sacudiendo las alas en la madrugada
declarando a voces el terror nocturno
perdiendo lentamente sus ropas en la caída.

El obispo saluda como saludan los valientes.

Las almas del purgatorio buscan su silla en el zaguán.

El obispo es una manzana de jade,
le brillan las costillas cuando sonríe
y cuando sonríe la lengua le estalla en llamas.
Obispo, obispo, tapado con albas servilletas
el amor es un cordón de aceite que va desde el vientre a la capilla.

Repicando está el sol
escondido entre los muebles
dudando ya del saber, sin taparrabo ni tabaco.

El amor se llena de una leche espesa
y la mañana cae de plano en los baldes de la pastora.

Si yo fuera verdugo arreglaría los cojines
en una jofaina de plata
la blanca mano recién cortada.

¿Por qué buscan los pastores la edad de oro
y no cuentan los malhadados sus corderos?

Y en el medio del río tu sentada como un brasero ardiendo.

THE FALL OF A BISHOP

Let the bells toll.
The bishop comes flying
shaking his wings in the morning dawn
yammering of the terrors of night
slowly losing his clothes as he falls.

The bishop is waving the way brave men wave.

The souls in purgatory look for their seats on the terrace.

The bishop is an apple of jade,
when he smiles his ribs shine
and his tongue breaks into flames when he smiles.
Bishop, oh Bishop, covered with snow-white napkins
love is a rope of oil flowing from your guts to the chapel.

The sun tolls
hidden among the furniture
still doubtful of knowledge, with neither a loincloth nor tobacco.

Love fills up with thick milk
and the morning falls straight into the buckets of the milkmaids.

If I were the hangman I'd arrange the velvet cushions
in a silver bowl
a white hand freshly cut.

Why are the shepherds still looking for the Golden Age
and why don't the miserable things count their sheep?

And in the middle of the river you sit like a burning coal.

La pequeña venganza queda a nuestra disposición.
Nos servimos los meses del año en un vaso
como una triste ilusión de novia ensangrentada.

Hemos comido demasiado:
una menta por ahí, un vientre por allá
una que otra carcajada
los tangos de Gardel.
Se me ha caído una pierna
una frasecilla en latín, una mirada en francés
en fin
sobre el pubis de la desdichada.

¿Y por qué de pronto comienzan a moverse las copas en la mesa?
¿Y por qué hacia ella? ¿Y por qué es todo predestinado y fijo
y feroz y desnudo?
¿Qué es la muerte?
La mirada torcida del emir en su baño de asiento.

Caen los sargentos del parrón
todo se ilumina.

No buscamos ya la madrugada a la vuelta de una esquina
la buscamos en su frente, en sus manos crispadas
en las sillas por el suelo, en la mujer de bruces
en el vino del ermitaño, en la bandera negra del fotógrafo
en la luz aposada en tu vientre
en el blanco seno que sube por la muralla
en la resignación de los suegros
en los pantalones a caballo sobre el bidet
en tu cabeza cortada
en la pregunta final.

¿Y dónde queda el cementerio de los pájaros?

Y en tu respuesta:
Te amaré a la caída de un obispo.

There's still a little vengeance left at our disposal.
We serve ourselves the months of the year in a glass
like the sad illusion of a bleeding bride.

We have eaten too much:
a mint here, a little piece there
one or two good laughs
Gardel's tangos.
I've dropped a leg
a few words of Latin, a glance in French
finally
over the pubis of the unlucky lady.

And why are the glasses suddenly moving on the table?
And why in her direction? And why is everything predestined and
    fixed
and naked and ferocious?
What is death?
The twisted grimace of the emir in his stiz bath.

The sergeants are falling from the trellis
and everything is lit up.

We don't look for the dawn around the corner any more
we look for it on his forehead, in his twitching hands
in the overturned chairs, in the woman face down
in the wine of the hermitage, in the black flag of the photographer
in the light sheltered in your belly
in the white breast climbing up the wall
in the resignation of the in-laws
in the pants lying straddled over the washtub
in your cut-off head
and in the final question.

And where is the cemetery of birds?

And in your answer:
I'll love you at the drop of a bishop.

Miguel Arteche

was born in 1926. He is the author of more than ten books of poetry and is the recipient of a number of awards. His works include *Una Nube, Otra Continente, Destierros y Tinieblas,* and *Para un Tiempo tan Breve.*

Yo sé que en esta lámpara apareces
y en la ceniza de este cigarillo,
y en el vaso, tal vez, me siento, escribo,
me oyes, y viajo, y vuelvo hacia otros meses.

Y aquí, bajo la lámpara en las eses
de soledad sin siempre sigues vivo,
mi muerto, mi sin mas mi adiós, mi amigo,
y sobre este papel desapareces.

Volví de nuevo hacia tu ayer: me llamas,
oigo tu voz de muerto en esa cinta,
la cinta que ya nunca me detiene

en esa casa oscura oscura casa,
y en esta negra tinta negra tinta,
y en estas blancas sienes blancas sienes.

I know that you are here in the lamplight,
in the ash of this cigarette, and in this glass;
you listen and watch me travel into the past
toward other days, as I sit here and write.

Now, in the light of this lamp we're always here
in the s's of endless loneliness I live
my death, my never more, farewell, my friend;
somewhere over the page you disappear.

On a tape that won't stop but still resounds
I can hear your dead voice calling me,
and I've gone back into your yesterday

in that house dark dark house,
in this black ink black ink,
in this hair gray hair gray.

José Donoso

was born in 1926 and is considered to be Chile's most prominent twentieth-century fiction writer. In his more than twelve books, which include novels, novelettes, and collections of short stories, his skill as a writer leads his readers into delightful worlds of the imagination, and so it is not surprising that he feels comfortable with the genre of poetry as well. His books, *El Obsceno Pájaro de la Noche, El Jardín de al Lado,* and *El Lugar sin Límites,* to name a few, are translated into English and other languages throughout Europe and the United States, as well as in South America.

Subió a decirnos Julia
que esta noche
Emilio mata el cerdo:
en cuanto oscurezca .
el crimen ceremonial
va a consàgrar el hambre.
Nos invitan
porque somos amigos.

El ritual sangriento se despliega
en la calle de estrecha y empinada escenografía;
ahita de fragancia del romero ardiendo;
juegan, violentos, los niños.
Las voces dirigiendo truenan:
date prisa, acorrálalo,
que no huya cuesta abajo;
que Espina acerque el fuego y traiga el cubo.
El forcejeo de los hombres
—más que el año pasado,
el doble que el del vecino—
iza al bruto sobre el ara:
manso en la mesa vieja de negra sangre y negro humo
y generaciones de agua hirviendo
que mata bestias ennobleciendo el pino.
Patalea—como si supiera—en medio de la calle
tan angosta, tan poblada,
tan cruel, tan íntima.

El chillido raja la oscuridad.
Se lo traga,

Julia came to tell us
that tonight
would be the pig-killing;
as soon as it was dusk
Emilio would direct the ritual kill
fulfilling the sacrament of hunger.
We were invited
because we were friends.

The bloody ceremony unfolds
in a narrow street buzzing with life,
loaded with the smell of burning rosemary
and children scuffling.
Voices give orders:
hurry, run him down,
don't let him go downhill;
get Porky to the fire and bring the bucket.
Sweating and struggling
"He's twice as big as last year's"
"bigger than the neighbors'"
they hoist the brute onto the slab
like a lamb on the old table, black with blood and soot
and generations of boiling water
for killing beasts, exalting man's first steps.
He flails the air—as if he knows—laid out in the middle of the street
so full, so confining,
so intimate, so cruel.

The scream rasps the darkness.
The darkness swallows it,

se escurre calzada abajo
con la sangre aguada entre las piedras.
Fallece por fin en el cielo estrecho
junto a nuestros gritos de triunfo.
Manos hurgan las entrañas,
codiciosas de residuos:
dedos hábiles, brazos teñidos
arrancan rizomas, glándulas, tripas.
Los abuelos adormecidos se animan:
visten su papel como un traje
porque otra muerte les devuelve la vida.
Madres viscerales cortan, anudan, vierten,
hunden manos sabias para organizar
lo que la muerte prepara
para consumirlo.
La breve agonía define propósitos fijos.
La muerte le da forma a todo,
como a los abanicos de piedra sobre las puertas
que desde tiempo inmemorial
dibujan la precisión del frío.

Los niños que yo conozco, allá,
temerían un aullido como este.
La noche angosta
no es proscenio adecuado para sus ritos.
Desconocen la relación entre dolor y hambre,
muerte y frío.
Pero los niños brutales de este invierno
conocen esos secretos y no los temen:
piedras, llamaradas de romero, guerra,
hambre y saciedad,
parra, ciprés, olivo.
Es la noche intemporal de los pueblos viejos
donde el hambre se combate con un cuchillo
y se habla del lobo que aúlla a la puerta
aunque agregan, orgullosos,
que ya no existe.

and it flows with the watery blood down the sidewalk
seeping between the rocks.
At last he dies under the narrow sky
surrounded by shouts of triumph.
They cut him open, poke at the entrails
fat with residue;
skillful fingers, blood-streaked arms
jerk out glands, organs, intestines.
Dozing grandfathers rouse up
donning paper aprons like Sunday suits.
Another death gives them new life.
The mothers are cutting, pouring, tying—
plunging hands trained to organize
what death prepares them to consume.
The brief agony has defined fixed goals.
Death gives order to everything,
even to the stone doorsills
that from the beginning of immemorable time
have outlined the precision of the cold.

Other children I know
would cry with fear at a scream like that one.
The narrow night
is not adequate for their rituals.
They can't envision the bond
between pain and hunger,
death and cold.
But the rough children of this winter
know its secrets and are not afraid:
rocks, blazing rosemary, war,
hunger, fulfillment, grapevine, cyprus, olive tree.
It's in the eternal night of all old towns
where hunger is fought with a knife
and they speak of the wolf who howls at the door,
and in the same breath, proudly
denounce him as a myth.

Otros cerdos familiares
mueren en otras calles,
reúnen o otros parientes, a otros amigos:
todos se comerán.
Eso basta.
Es preciso que el frío se apacigüe adentro,
en el vientre,
hecho un nudo bajo el umbligo
para que el grito se transforme,
como a muerte, en refugio tibio:
igual que en la noche de la alcoba
el abrazo de los padres esboza un dolor
que no los desvela con la trivial certeza
de que es parecido al dolor gozoso
con que fueron paridos.

Despertamos a la superficie pulida
del siguiente día:
el sol intenta hurgar en las hondas calles
sus sombras breves, partidas.
Son los juegos,
el calor que se lleva adentro por lo comido,
lo que calienta la tarde de los niños
y alienta sus violencias de juguete y sus trinos.
A mí, este invierno europeo,
tan largo, tan distinto,
me astilla el corazón y las manos.
Ya no soy el mismo.
Sucumben la anécdota y la metáfora.
El recuerdo embiste,
se parte contra esta dureza sin alterarla:
queda resonando en el frío largo
del invierno distinto,
este hambre apaciguado
como un chillido doméstico y terrible.

Other pigs, brothers, cousins
die in other streets,
joining their friends and neighbors;
all will be eaten.
That is enough.
It is right for the cold to be appeased
down in the belly,
making a knot below the navel
so that the scream be transformed,
like death, into a warm refuge;
like a night in the cave
the parents' embrace is a rough draft of the pain
that does not reveal them the simple certainty
of its likeness to that delicious pain
that stood them on their feet.

We wake up to the polished surface
of the next day.
In the deep streets, the sun tries to stir up
the quick, broken shadows.
These are the games:
the warmth carried within us by the eaten,
heating the children's afternoon
giving vigor to their rough games and songs.
As for me, this European winter,
so long, so different from that other one,
cracks my hands and my heart.
I'm not the same now.
Story and metaphor have died.
Memory rushes to attack,
shattering against this hardness without hurting it,
and hangs resounding in the air of the enduring cold
from the other winter,
this pacified hunger
like a tamed scream, domestic and terrible.

Enrique Lihn

is a painter, poet, short-story writer, and essayist. He was born in Santiago in 1929 and studied at the Escuela de Bellas Artes where he earned many awards for his paintings. Later, he received numerous awards for his writing including the *Pedro de Ona,* the *Casa de las Americas,* the *Municipal de Cuento,* and the *Municipal de Poesía.* He has published more than fourteen books; among the most recent are *A Partir de Manhattan, El Arte de la Palabra, Derechos del Autor,* and *Al Bello Aperecer de este Lucero.*

NADA QUE VER EN LA MIRADA

Un mundo de voyeurs sabe que la mirada
es sólo un escenario
donde el espectador se mira en sus fantasmas
Un mundo de voyeurs no mira lo que ve
sabe que la mirada no es profunda
y se cuida muy bien de fojarla o clavarla
Entre desconocidos nadie aquí mira a nadie
No miro a la Gioconda
ni a Einstein en el subway
En eso de mirar hay un peligro inútil
fuera de que no hay nada que ver en la mirada.

NOTHING TO SEE AT A GLANCE

Everyone knows that a glance
is a stage
the spectator looking at his own phantom
Everyone knows we don't look at what we see
knowing a glance is not important
careful to fasten it
on strangers no one here looks at anyone
I don't look at the Mona Lisa
nor at Einstein on the subway
There is a futile danger in the act of looking
anyway there's nothing to see at a glance.

ESCOMBRO

Sus sueños de grandeza no concluyeron
hasta el día en que cayó no enfermo, loco
allí, en el reino de la miseria, y se estuvo
entonces acostumbrando a lo que ya nunca dejaría
de ocurrirle, arrastrándolos pesadamente
—esos sueños—como a los cadáveres el celador nocturno en
       la morgue.
La idiotez ulterior
y su nueva mujer con la que se conocía en una clínica
como salvada—llena de tizne—del derrumbe de un incendio
       en el Bronx
donde se mata a las casas con fuego
un dolor de cabeza que lo obliga a desistir en seguida
de la más mínima lectura
y a vender sus libros ilegibles al menudo
entre amigos que con razón preferirían no verlo
sus inoportunas llamadas telefónicas a cuenta del receptor
       en horas del amanecer
silenciosas o como si fueran
todo eso y la comodidad, por fin, del escombro humano
lo han hecho echar raíces en las proximidades del Reino
cerca de la locura.

TRASH

His dreams finally came true
the day that he went mad
there in the kingdom of misery
he grew reconciled to what would never happen
dragging out those dreams
like a mortician dragging bodies
       out of the morgue.
That inward lunacy,
the new woman he'd met in the clinic
a seared piece of human salvage, rescued
       from the rubble of a fire in the Bronx
where old houses are put to death by burning
a pain in his head that won't let him read
for any length of time
pushing his incomprehensible books for pennies
to friends who understandably try to avoid him
his bothersome collect calls
       at all hours of the night
wordless or the same as
all this and the comforts of a life of trash
have led him to put down roots in the neighborhood
of that kingdom very close to madness.

LEONES DEL NOVECIENTOS

El león, un buen padre de familia
tierno a brutal según el viento que sople
domable, es cierto, pero nunca servil
fue el modelo ideal del siglo diecinueve.
Todos los escultores hicieron de los circos
su taller—empezando por los peores falsarios
(los pequeños felinos del arte de agradar).
Millones de leones fueron movilizados
desde la selva al mundo del vaciado en metal
Rugió el mármol, la piedra se puso leonina
Por cientos y por miles
leones de artificio se esparcieron
por la ciudad, subiendo
de dos en dos las gradas de todos los palacios
y allí montaron guardia en nombre de la Ley
Pero no eran leones ni exactamente perros
eran los carceleros de sí mismos, los amos
del Poder pavoneándose en forma de león.

LIONS OF THE NINETEENTH CENTURY

The lion, good family father
tender, or brutal, according to the trend
not indomitable, but never tamed
was the top model of the nineteenth century.
The sculptors made the circus their studio
beginning with the poorest counterfeits
(those little felines so pleasing to everyone).
Then millions of lions were taken from the jungle
into the die-cast metal world.
The marble roared; the stones turned leonine
for miles and by the hundreds
artificial lions cropped up
in all the cities, climbing
two by two up the steps of palaces
standing guard there in the name of the Law
but they weren't lions or even watch dogs exactly
They were their own wardens
swaggering landlords of power in lion form.

Delia Domínguez

was born in 1931 and is one of Chile's southern poets. Her poetry reflects the imagery and traditions of that locale, with themes centering around love and death, joy, and memories. Among her major works are *La Tierra nace al Canto*, *Contracanto*, and *El Sol mira para atrás*. And recently, she has also published some scholarly works about Chilean and Mexican folklore and customs.

LA VIDA ESTA EN LA CALLE

La vida está en la calle del pueblo
entre el correo y el mercado
y la parroquería San Mateo.
La vida está en la calle como la muerte
y eso lo sabe cualquiera
con dos dedos de frente.
Yo la aprendo
cuando la puestera con sus 85
ofrece hierbas con recetas de amor
cuando en la herrería de F. Cardenas
la camisa
ampara los sueños sagrados de la infancia.
o con Melián en su talabartería
entre pellones y monturas
hablando de los cueros buenos y malos
porque todo tiene su lado
como la ira o la razón.
Y la aprendo
cuando asoma la Ana Torres
con la cabeza crespa y sus crisántemos
tan dorados como los ojos de Dios
                    o de su niño recibido,
y me pide lecturas porque no sabe leer
mientras la hora se la llevan los pájaros
a las tolvas de la Companía Molinera
y un santo aroma de pan y levaduras
viene a entibiar la casa.

Y la Ana
defendiendo sus florerías y sus huesos

LIFE IS IN THE STREET

Life is in the street
between the post office and the market place
and St. Matthew's Chapel.
Life is in the street like death
even a half-wit knows that
I learn about it
from the 85-year-old peddler woman
calling out her herbs and love potions,
and from Cardenas' blacksmith shop
where the furnace shelters the sacred dreams of childhood,
from Melian at the saddlery
surrounded by hides and saddletrappings
and talking of good leathers and bad
since everything has its place
like fury and reason.
I learn about it
from Ana Torres when she comes out
with her curly hair and her chrysanthemums
golden as the eyes of God
                        or the Son of God,
and she asks me for stories because she can't read.
Meanwhile birds wing the hour
to the hoppers of the village bakery
where a sacred aroma of yeast comes pouring out
and freshens the house.

Ana, too
defending her flowers and her bones

desde la ventanilla de su kiosko
me enseña
el calor que juntaba para el hijo dormido
antes de su primera muerte. Después,
ella sola
tú solo
la eternidad marcada por los símbolos.

Así aprendo la vida
en la pizarra dura de la tierra
donde va a quedar mi última voluntad.

from the window of her kiosk
shows me
with the fire she is kindling for her sleeping son
saving it up for his first death.
Then, she alone,
you alone,
eternity marked by symbols.

That's how I'm learning life
on the hard blackboard of the land
where I shall leave my last will and testament.

Carlos Cortínez

was born in Santiago in 1934. For some years, he was one of the main editors of the poetic journal *Trilce,* published in Santiago by Editorial Universitaria. In addition to his poetry, *Opus Cero* and *Treinta y Tres,* for example, he is also known for his critical essays, both in Chile and in the United States. His most recent critical work, *Borges the Poet,* was published by The University of Arkansas Press. He presently resides in Pennsylvania where he is a professor at Fairleigh Dickinson College.

AQUI HAY ALGUN ERROR

Comí anoche con Beethoven.
Ustedes lo conocen,
corpulento y ya algo sordo.

Se bebió bastante vino
y a los postres
puse en la gramola
toda una pastoral
(no pretendía originalidades).

Bastó que él distinguiera algunas notas
se alzó airado entre el cognac
y dijo:
        —¿cómo es esto
si aún no escribo esta sinfonía!

Tranquilízate Ludwig . . .
tú no oyes
yo no entiendo
tu idioma
y ocupamos siglos diferentes . . .

Devolvió el vino
        y se fue.

THERE'S BEEN A SLIGHT MISTAKE

Last night I dined with Beethoven.
You may know him,
a little on the fat side and somewhat deaf.

He drank too much wine
and then for dessert
I put on a record
of a pastoral
(it didn't boast originality).

It was enough for him to make out a few notes
furious he jumped up, glass in hand
and said:
        "What's this!
I haven't written that symphony yet!"

Calm yourself Ludwig . . .
you're deaf
we don't speak
the same language
we live in different centuries . . .

He handed me his wine
        and he left.

Jorge Teillier

is a well-known poet who established himself in the sixties along with Lihn and Arteche and other poets of his generation. Born in 1935, he is the author of more than ten books of poetry; the more recently published are *El Pasajero del Hotel Usher,* and *Cartas para reinas de otras primaveras.* A collection of his select works was published by Editorial Universitaria, entitled *Muertes y maravillas.*

DESPUES DE TODO

Después de todo
nos volveremos a encontrar.
El verano tenderá sus manteles en el suelo
para que dispongamos nuestras provisiones
y tú seguirás bella
como la canción *El Vino de Mediodía*
que el loco tocaba en la leñera.

Después de todo
hay tantas y tantas tierras.
Yo no me impaciento.
Tenemos todos los años del mundo para recorrerlas
hasta que de nuevo estemos juntos
y tú me contarás
que una vez me conociste
en un pequeño planeta que yo no recuerdo
un planeta llamado Tierra
y vas a hablarme
de casas visitadas por la luna,
billetes de apuesta a los hipódromos,
nuestros iniciales dibujadas con tiza blanca
          en un muro en demolición.

Equivoquémonos todo lo que queramos.
La tierra de desamor no existe
ante el gesto tuyo de mostrar las magnolias
          de una plaza de barrio
tu cabeza en mi hombro
la clara música nocturna de tu cuerpo.

WHEN ALL IS SAID AND DONE

We'll be together again
when all's said and done.
The summer will lay its blanket on the ground
for us to spread our picnic
and you will still be as beautiful
as "Wine at Noon,"
the song that the crazy man used to sing in the woodshed.

There are so many lands
when all is said and done.
I'll be patient.
We have eternity to run through them
until we're together again
and you tell me
that you knew me once
on a small planet that I can't remember
called Earth
and you speak to me
of houses visited by the moon,
two-dollar tickets at the hippodrome,
our initials scrawled in chalk
        on a wall about to be torn down.

We'll find out we were wrong about what we wanted.
The land of indifference is wiped out
by your gesture when you show me the magnolias
        on the town square
your head on my shoulder
the sweet night song of your body.

Un gesto rehace todo:
cuando la casa se incendia
su vida sigue entera
en la hoja chamuscada de un cuaderno,
el alfil sobreviviente del ajedrez.

En otro lugar,
lejos de esta tierra y de su tiempo
espero tu rostro
donde se reúnen todos los rostros que he amado,
y comenzaremos a ser otra vez los desconocidos
que hace años se miraban y miraban
sin atraverse a decir que iban a amarse.

A gesture brings it all back again;
When a house burns
its life goes on
in the charred pages of a notebook,
in the last surviving bishop of a chess game.

Somewhere else,
far from this time and place,
I'll wait for your face
where it will join those others that I have loved,
and we'll start all over again as strangers
who have gazed at one another for years and years
not daring to speak of loving.

PARA HABLAR CON LOS MUERTOS

Para hablar con los muertos
hay que elegir palabras
que ellos reconozcan tan fácilmente
como sus manos
reconocían el pelaje de sus perros en la oscuridad.
Palabras claras y tranquilas
como el agua del torrente domesticada en la copa
o las sillas ordenadas por la madre
después que se han ido los invitados.
Palabras que la noche acoja
como a los fuegos fatuos los pantanos.

Para hablar con los muertos
hay que saber esperar:
ellos son miedosos
como los primeros pasos de un niño.
Pero si tenemos paciencia
un día nos responderán
con una hoja de álamo atrapado por un espejo roto,
con una llama de súbito reanimada en la chimenea,
con un regreso oscuro de pájaros
frente a la mirada de una muchacha
que aguarda inmóvil en el umbral.

TO SPEAK WITH THE DEAD

To speak with the dead
you must choose your words carefully
words they will know
the way their hands know
the form of a dog in the dark.
Clear, soft words
like rainwater caught in a cup.
Like chairs put back in their places
after the guests have gone.
Words which the night will contain
the way a swamp contains its foolish fires.

To speak with the dead
you must learn how to wait;
they are timid
as a baby with his first steps.
If you are patient
one day they will answer
with a poplar leaf trapped in a broken mirror,
with a sudden leap of flame in the fireplace,
with a dark flutter of birds returning,
passing in front of a girl who watches
motionless in the doorway.

LEWIS CARROLL

Un profesor de matemáticas de Oxford
El Reverendo Dodgson
Ligeramante tartamudo y zurdo
Nos deja en la primera casilla de otro mundo
Allí para el unicornio somos monstruos fabulosos
Y se oye el ruido de armaduras
De caballeros que piensan mejor cuando están cabeza abajo

El señor Dodgson pasea con tres niñitas
Tal vez sueña fotografiarlas desnudas
Pero estamos en el siglo xix
En plena Era Victoriana
Y se contenta con escribirlas cartas festivas
Con narrarles historias
Sobre el otro lado del espejo
Y ver fluir sus tiernos rostros en el atardecer de una barca

El nombre Alicia significa ahora Aventura
Y cuando lleguemos a la octava casilla
Empezaremos a ser reyes
En un juego que ya no vamos a olvidar

LEWIS CARROLL

A professor of mathematics at Oxford
Reverend Dodgson by name
A little deaf with a slight stutter
Leaves us on the first square of a world
Where to the unicorn we are mythical beasts
And in the distance you hear sounds of battle
From knights who think better upside down

Mr. Dodgson takes walks with three little girls
He may dream of photographing them in the nude
But this is the 19th century
The height of the Victorian Era
So he must content himself with writing them silly letters
And telling them stories
About the other side of the mirror
And watching their sweet faces mirrored from a boat at twilight

The name of Alice means Adventure now
When we finally reach the last square
We will all be kings and queens
In a game that none of us will ever forget

Armando Uribe Arce

was born in 1935. Some of his poetic works include *Engañoso Laúd* and *No Hay Lugar*. His poetry has been translated into French and English.

POEMAS

Los cantos de los niños
como una llama crecen.
Los jovenes desean
gozar. Los dioses soplan.

———

Ser un niño que mira un agujero
sin conocer el término agujero.

———

Los niños no me dicen
nada, Busco a un anciano.
Los ancianos a punto
de morir me hacen: chiiit.

———

Camines donde camines
adonde camines
caminarás a la tumba
caminarás en la tumba.

———

Sé lo que digo. Digo
que no sé lo que digo.

———

POEMS

The children's songs
grow like a flame.
The young want pleasure.
The gods blow.

———

To be a little child looking down a hole
without knowing the word hole.

———

The children can't tell me anything;
I look for an old man.
The old men on their deathbeds
tell me, "Bah!"

———

Walk where you want to walk
wherever you walk
you're walking toward your grave
you're walking on your grave.

———

I know what I say. I say
I don't know what I say.

———

La sabiduría es difícil,
difícil la ignorancia.
Descender al detalle?
Ascender al detalle.

—

No quiero nada con nadie.
No quiero decir repito.
No quiero nada repito.

—

¿Quién recibe al poeta en este mundo?
Viven como ratones perseguidos
por gatos perseguidos
por perros perseguidos por su cola.

—

¿Cómo huir de quien me sigue, cómo huir
si lo sigo y clamo y deseo que me halle.

—

O, si fuéramos ambos
árboles inconscientes.

—

Yo le paso los ojos
y ella cruza los pies como distintos sexos.

—

Y sé que soy el mismo que a los trece
o quince años mintió a Dios diciendo
no soy más que gusanos y carroña
y era un niño y las flores daban fruta!

—

Wisdom is hard,
ignorance hard.
Get down to details?
Rise up to details.

———

I don't want anything to do with anyone.
I don't want to say I repeat.
I don't want anything I repeat.

———

Who takes in the poets of this world?
They live like rats chased
by cats chased
by dogs chased by their tails.

———

How to escape from what is after me, how to escape
if I chase it down and shout at it and force it to find me.

———

Oh, that we were both
unconscious trees.

———

I run my eyes over her
she crosses her ankles like opposite sexes.

———

I know I'm the same one who lied to God
at thirteen or fifteen saying
I'm nothing but worms and rot
but really I was a boy and blossoms were bearing fruit!

———

En el principio estaba, Dios mío, quién estaba?
el verbo ser y el verbo estar estaban
colgados de una escobilla de dientes
¡qué original, que mentiroso!

y estaba el espíritu invisible
creando cosas como un loco,
sacándoselas de la manga como un manco.

———

No quiero ser ejemplo
de nadie ni ludibrio
de nadie. Bajo un grán
diccionario me escondo.

In the beginning was, my God, who was?
the verb to exist and the verb to be were
hanging from a toothbrush
how original, how false!

the invisible spirit was
creating things like mad
shaking them out of his sleeve like a one-armed magician.

———

I don't want to be
an example of anyone
nor a mockery of anyone. I'll hide
under a giant dictionary.

David Turkeltaub

was born in 1936. He has published several books of poetry, including *Hombre-cito Verde* and *Códices*. A more recent book is entitled *Los Arrepentimientos*. His work has also appeared in anthologies. Presently, he lives in Santiago where he is the director and editor of Editorial Ganymedes, a publishing house specializing in select poetry collections of the most outstanding Chilean poets.

LA MUERTE
INTERRUMPE LA RUTINA

Sala espesa de
culebras
colgando el
silbido
del teléfono
me vestí
como pude
       salí
a tropezones
a la calle
caminé sin parar
ya estaba blanca
fría
alguien me dió café
cargué la pipa me ocupé de los detalles
encontré fotos borradores
me solté a llorar a todo trapo
por qué yo para qué
sobreviviente
son recién las cinco veinticinco
no sé si ir a la oficina
hay que avisar a pedro y a fulano
¡zumba! cómo molestan los muertos.

DEATH
INTERRUPTS ROUTINE

Living room
heavy
with snakes
the telephone
rings
I get dressed
as best I can
         go
stumbling
into the street
walk without stopping
it was cold already
and white
someone gives me coffee
I fill my pipe busy myself with details
find some faded pictures
break down and cry for a while
why me what for
survivor
only just turned five twenty-five
I don't know if I should go by the office
I would have to tell every Tom, Dick, and Harry
damn it all! the dead are troublesome.

DE PRONTO COMPRENDI

De pronto comprendí que me habían asesinado:
lancéme entonces a recorrer las calles,
mis calles habituales, preguntando,
los cafés, los domicilios de todos mis amigos,
coincidiendo:
no, señor, no lo hemos visto,
tiempo ha que no aparece,
se fue llevándose mis ágatas,
necesito hablar con él de ciergas cosas
y así por el estilo y el estilo.

A medianoche, cansadísimo,
tomé el último café de la jornada.

SUDDENLY I UNDERSTOOD

Suddenly I understood that they had killed me.
In a frenzy I began to walk the streets,
my streets, asking
at the bars, at the homes of friends,
getting:
no, man, we haven't seen him,
it's been a while since he's been here,
he made off with some of my stuff,
I need to get hold of him
and so on and so forth etc.

Around midnight, dead tired,
I sipped the last coffee of the day.

INFORME DEL TIEMPO

Hay una persona que ya no sirve para nada
la taparon con diarios para esconder esta pálida
      vergüenza
oh gritaron todos los periodistas
morir es una experiencia inolvidable

cae una lluvia fina desganada
lo que se llama una llovizna
los días se muerden la cola
pero el resto del país está tranquilo

la poesía se sienta a la diestra de dios
y espera las noticias

hay una gotera en el cielo

pero el resto del país está tranquilo.

NEWSCAST

There is a human being who is totally useless now
they drop newspapers over him to cover his pallid
        embarrassment
oh cried all the reporters
dying is such an unforgettable experience

a listless rain is falling
they call it a drizzle
the days are chasing their tails
but all the rest of the country is at peace

poetry is sitting at the right hand of God
waiting for news

there is a leak in the sky

but all the rest of the country is at peace.

CARTA ABIERTA

Y cuatro tapadas.
Me juego entero al diez que veo.

Me encontré a mí mismo,
me saludé.
La suerte me sonríe,
la vecina no.
Tuvo razón la radio cuando dijo
que en otoño París es una lluvia
de elefantes melancólicos.

Veo un ocho, un seis,
un nueve.
Me juego el todo
por el todo por el siete.

UPTURNED CARD

And four face down
I bet everything on the ten showing.

I meet myself;
I greet myself.
Luck smiles on me,
not the woman beside me.
The radio was right when it said that in autumn
Paris is raining elephants
sad elephants.

I show an eight, a six,
a nine.
I stake the whole pile
on a seven.

LA POESIA SIRVE PARA TODO

La poesía sirve para todo: reemplaza a la anestesia
donde el dentista, y no produce efectos secundarios.
En dosis muy concentradas (p.ej. Keats + Vallejo) puede dar
        escalofríos en la médula espinal,
estremecimientos, palidéz
y una sensación de pisar en el vació.
En esos casos se recomienda dejar una flor seca entre las hojas
señalando al culpable—hasta que otra alma piadosa
de aquí a cien años
arriesgue el pellejo en la aventura.

POETRY IS GOOD FOR ANYTHING

Poetry is good for anything: it replaces anesthesia
at the dentist's, with no side effects.
In concentrated doses (i.e., Keats + Vallejo)
      it causes chills down the spine,
trembling, blanching,
a sensation of walking on air.
In such cases you should press a flower between the leaves
to mark the page responsible—until some daring soul
a hundred years from now
risks his neck in the same adventure.

Como el último bloque de concreto para terminar la escollera
el mar trae refuerzos trae de lejos señoritas emperifolladas
cuanto tiempo perdido subiendo escaleras esperando omnibuses
novias fui fotógrafo especializado en novias recalcitrantes
y el tiempo perdido esperando el agua más fresca de la llave
a quien no le dan sed los matrimonios una cansada barcarola
pero me queda el tiempo ganado en las tómbolas de balnearios
el héroe desnudo muerto del rasguño de una verja herrumbrada
sus compañeras pálidas juntan sol en el umbligo la pianista
era un elefante gris claro un claro elefante gris clavecín
solo me queda el tiempo ganado en las tómbolas de balnearios
la oscura ecuanimidad del que reparte el barro de la acequia
como si fuera el último blockque de concreto en la escollera

Like the last block of concrete set into the breakwater the sea brings reinforcements brings from thousands of miles young ladies in beautiful dresses all that time wasted climbing stairs waiting for buses brides I specialized in photographing balky brides and all that time wasted waiting for water fresh from the tap what wedding wouldn't make anyone thirsty a tired gondola serenade but still I gained some time from the lottery tables at the spa the naked hero dead from the scratch of a rusty rail his pale companions are tanning their belly buttons the piano player was a gray elephant that's right a light gray elephant pianist all I have left is the time gained from the lottery tables at the spa and the dark placid measure of the mud from the drainage ditch as if it would be the last block of concrete in the breakwater

Oscar Hahn

was born in 1938 and is currently a professor of Spanish literature at the University of Iowa in Iowa City. His major works include *Mal de Amor,* which earlier appeared as *La Rosa Negra,* and *Arte de Morir.* His poetry was also published in *Ganymedes 6,* an anthology of contemporary Chilean poetry published by Editorial Ganymedes.

EL CENTRO DEL DORMITORIO

Un ojo choca contra las torres del sueño
y se queja por cada uno de sus fragmentos
mientras cae la nieve en las calles de Iowa City
la triste nieve la nieve sucia de hogaño

Algo nos despertó en medio de la noche
quizás un pequeño salto un pequeño murmullo
posiblemente los pasos de una sombra en el césped
algo difícil de precisar pero flotante

Y aquello estaba allí: de pie en el centro del dormitorio
con una vela sobre la cabeza
y la cera rodándole por las mejillas

Ahora me levanto ahora voy al baño ahora tomo agua
ahora me miro en el espejo: y desde el fondo
eso también nos mira
con su cara tan triste con sus ojos llenos de cera
mientras cae la nieve en el centro del dormitorio
la triste nieve la nieve sucia de hogaño

IN THE MIDDLE OF THE BEDROOM

An eye crashes against the towers of a dream
and whines for its broken pieces
while the snow falls on the streets of Iowa City
the sad snow the dirty snow of these winter days

Something wakes us up in the middle of the night
maybe a slight toss or a slight murmur
the footfalls perhaps of a shadow on the lawn
something difficult to describe but floating

And there it is, standing in the middle of the bedroom
with a veil over its head
and wax rolling down its cheeks

I get up now I go to the bathroom I take a drink of water
I look at myself in the mirror; from the depths of it
that thing looks back at us
with its sad, sad face with its eyes full of wax
while the snow falls in the middle of the bedroom
the sad snow the dirty snow of these winter days

DON JUAN

Todas estas mujeres que rodean
el lecho donde yazgo cada día
son un coro de velas carnosísimas
pero se van en fila retirando
y estoy solo otra vez en el espacio
del mundo y ahora pasan lentamente
por mi lecho de nuevo pero no
aunque estás a mi lado respirando
con tantas bocas tantos ojos múltiples
locamente y yo miro el cielo raso
y el lecho donde yazgo cada día
mientras todas las bellas van poniendo
flores blancas sobre este pobre cuerpo
que me cubren de arena que me cubren
de arena blanca y respirar no puedo
en mi lecho caliente circundado
por mujeres que rezan y que lloran

DON JUAN

All these women gathered around
the bed where I lie all day long
are a choir of carnal night angels
but then they go away in single file
and I'm left alone again in space
and in the world and now they float slowly
by my bed again but no
even though you are beside me breathing crazily
with so many mouths so many multiple eyes
I'm staring at the plain sky
and at this bed where I lie all day long
while all the beautiful women come and lay
white flowers on my poor body
let them cover me with sand let them cover me
with white sand I can't breathe
in my hot bed surrounded
by women praying, crying

GLADIOLOS JUNTO AL MAR

Gladíolos rojos de sangrantes plumas,
lenguas del campo, llamas olorosas,
de las olas azules, amorosas,
cartas os llegan, pálidas espumas.

Flotan sobre las alas de las brumas
epístolas de polen numerosas,
donde a las aguas piden por esposas
gladíolos rojos de sangrantes plumas.

Movidas son las olas por el viento
y el pie de los gladíolos van besando,
al son de un suave y blando movimiento.
Y en cada dulce flor de sangre inerte
la muerte va con piel de sal entrando,
y entrando van las flores en la muerte.

GLADIOLAS BY THE SEA

Gladiolas with plumes like blood,
fragrant flame-tongues of the field,
from the sea to you, amorous waves yield
white sea-foam, letters of love.

On the waves' wings, floating in the flood
of tide, the full pollen sacks ride,
asking the waters for a bride
from the gladiolas with plumes like blood.

Tenderly kissing the red flowers' feet,
the waves are wafted forward by the wind
to the sound of a movement soft and sweet,
and as into each fragrant blood flower,
death comes seeping with salty skin,
so they seep into death hour by hour.

Hernán Lavín Cerda

was born in 1939. His work has appeared in numerous anthologies. His volumes of poetry include *La Conspiración*, *Ciegamente los ojos*, and *Ceremonias de Afaf*.

MEJOR EL FUEGO

Deja que las moscas
sigan explicando el mundo en su manera.
Al fín todo se ordena y hasta las moscas
     se explican solas:
            —La luz
pierde su vida detrás de la luz:
los astrónomos son perseguidos por las bestias.
La luz se pierde de vista y las tortugas
                    verdes
vienen a morir sobre la arena.

AHORA CUELGAS
COMO UN COLLAR EN RUINAS

Es inútil que te pintes los ojos y los labios
No te pongas delante del espejo
No te acerques
Aléjate
Ya es demasiado tarde y el anillo de jade
no te dará la buena suerte
La vida no ha pasado en vano
Y ahora cuelgas como un collar en ruinas
Te compadezco
Por tí no hice nada que valiera la pena
Te doy lástima

BETTER THE FIRE

Let the flies
go on explaining the world in their own way.
Everything, in the end, will be in order
right down to the flies:
$\qquad\qquad$ "the light
fades in light"
the astronomers are chased by monsters.
The light fades out and the green
$\qquad\qquad\qquad\qquad$ turtles
come to die upon the sand.

NOW YOU HANG
LIKE A BROKEN NECKLACE

It's no use putting on all that make-up
Don't stand so close to the mirror
Don't even look into it
Back off
It's too late now and that jade ring of yours
won't bring you good luck any more
We don't live this life for nothing
But now you hang like a broken necklace
I pity you
I never did much for you
And that's a shame

LA CALAVERA

Nada se puede medir:
                    solo es exacta
la velocidad de la sombra
donde tu calavera
                    se ilumina

La calavera
            esconde su lengua
y me sonríe:
              yo me estiro la punta de pie
y dejo caer una moneda
en su hocico

BEGONIAS

El sol
cruza la puerta de la casa
                          en una begonia.
El sol como el polvo húmedo
por la cercanía del pozo.
                    El deseo
como el pozo
            donde el sol se aleja de sí mismo.
  —Toda begonia es un crimen.

THE SKULL

Nothing can be measured;
                    the only true preciseness
is the speed of the shadow
where your skull
           shines

The skull
        hides its tongue
and grins at me;
           I stand on tip-toe
and drop a coin
into its snout

BEGONIAS

The sun
crosses the threshold
              on a begonia,
The sun like damp dust
through the proximity of a pond.
                   Desire
like the pond
        where the sun fades out.
        —every begonia is a crime.

133

DESTIERRO

Cuando todos se vayan,
deberemos desenterrar los huevos de pingüino:
¿Quién derramó el aceite
                      de las focas?
El árbol del agua: el agua del exilio.
¿Quién estrelló las uvas contra la ventana?
Toda boda es un destierro como el huevo
  de Colón.

UNEARTHING

When everyone leaves,
we must dig up the penguin eggs;
Who has spilled
            the seal oil?
Tree of water; water of exile
Who threw the grapes against the window?
Every wedding is an unearthing like the egg
           of Columbus.

Manuel Silva Acevedo

was born in 1942 and presently resides in Las Vertienes. His work has appeared in journals and anthologies. His first book, *Perterbaciones,* was published in 1967, and *Lobos y ovejas,* published in 1976, obtained the Oyarzuen Award, sponsored by the journal *Trilce. Mester de bastardía* obtained the Libro de Oro Poetry Award in 1977. *Monte de Venus* was published in 1979. Silva's poetry has been translated into German, Dutch, and French.

His work is similar to both that of Turkeltaub and Gonzalo Rojas. Sometimes it is strongly philosophical and analytical. In addition to love themes in his poetry, many of Silva's poems are about death.

CONTRA NATURA

Ven y toca, me dijo la vieja
y me ofreció los pechos
Ayer un hombre reclinó en ellos su cabeza
y los llamó rosas, jazmines, coronas de espinas.

SUEÑO

Soñé que un automóvil arrollaba a un hombre
Hoy abrí el diario
y vi la foto de un hombre arrollado por un automóvil
y al volver a mi casa por la noche
vi un automóvil arrollar a un hombre
En ese instante me tocaron el hombro y al volverme
alguien dijo: acompáñeme a la policía!

CONTRARY TO NATURE

Come and feel, the old woman said
and she offered me her breasts
Yesterday, a man rested his head against them
and he called them roses, jasmines, a crown of thorns.

DREAM

Last night I dreamed that a car ran over a man
This morning I picked up the newspaper
and saw the picture of a man run over by a car
As I was going home in the evening
I saw a man run over by a car
Then someone tapped me on the shoulder and I turned around.
"You're under arrest," they said.

QUE RUEDE LA CABEZA DEL POETA

El poeta ya no cree en nada.
Va por mal camino.
Lleva la mochila vacía.
Se ha puesto de rodillas.
Pide limosna a gritos.
Agotó los últimos recursos.
Su barba está llena de parásitos.
La muerte lo visita con frecuencia.
Ya no sabe de nada.

Que ruede la cabeza del poeta.

OFF WITH THE POET'S HEAD

The poet doesn't believe in anything anymore.
He's taken the wrong road.
He's carrying an empty pack on his back.
He's down on his knees.
He cries for alms at the top of his lungs.
He's exhausted all his resources.
His beard is full of parasites.
Death has been seeing him a lot lately.
He doesn't know anything anymore.

Off with the poet's head!

LA RATA

Cuando esa noche sentí la roedura de la Rata, supe que algo malo nos iba a pasar, esto que nos pasa. Por eso no quise despertarte ni a la mañana siguiente te dije nada.

Cuando esa noche sentiste la roedura de la Rata, supiste que algo malo nos iba a pasar, esto que nos pasa. Por eso fingiste estar dormida y a la mañana siguiente no me dijiste nada.

Cuando esa noche la Rata se introdujo en nuestra madriguera y se puso a roer, supo que algo malo nos iba a pasar, esto que nos pasa. Por eso siguió royendo obstinada y desapareció al llegar la mañana.

Y ahora que está pasando esto que nos pasa, culpo a la Rata que en vez de abandonarlo invadió nuestro barco que se hundía. Y culpo a las cancerosas palomas de mal agüero que revoloteaban sobre los tejados vecinos, a esas siniestras mensajeras de una paz humillante.

Y culpo al día malo en que tu grito me aterró bajo la lluvia del baño, cuando corrí a socorrerte desnudo como un mono de las cavernas sin más armas que mis manos precarias.

E insisto en culpar a la Rata que me señalaste oculta tras un mueble. Culpo al temblor de mis manos con que cogí esa escoba miserable y empujé el armario para enfrentar a nuestra enemiga. Culpo al fatalismo que se me encasquetó al descargar el primer golpe sabiendo que no daría. Culpo a la ciega torpeza con que removí todos los muebles de la sala asestando golpes fallidos. Yo me culpo de haberle despejado el camino a nuestra habitación, donde todo estaría perdido. Me culpo de haberla obligado a ocultarse entre nuestras ropas, entre estas ropas. Me inculpo de haberte permitido participar en la grotesca cacería tambien tú armada de un escobajo. Pero sobre todo me acuso de haber errado el golpe decisivo, ese que tú le diste a la Rata hembra preñada, porque entonces comenzó a pasar esto que nos pasa, cuando me descubrí desnudo carne de gallina con un palo en la mano a guisa de adarga y con la Rata muerta cogida por la cola, mirándote, sintiéndome mirado por tus vidriosos ojos de Rata, de cuyo hociquito fluía un hilillo de sangre.

THE RAT

That night, when I heard the gnawing of the Rat, I knew something bad was going to happen to us, what's happening now. That's why I didn't want to wake you, why I didn't say anything the next day.

That night, when you heard the gnawing of the Rat, you knew something bad was going to happen to us, what's happening now. That's why you pretended to be asleep, why you didn't say anything the next day.

That night, when the Rat intruded into the den and started gnawing, it knew something bad was going to happen to us, what's happening now. That's why it kept on gnawing and disappeared the next day.

Now that what is happening to us is happening to us, I blame the Rat; instead of leaving, it boarded our sinking ship. I blame those nasty pigeons; evil omens, they kept flying around the neighbors' roofs, harbingers of a contemptible peace.

I blame the mean day, when your scream filled me with terror in the shower, and I ran out naked to help you, like a monkey out of his cave, armed with nothing but my slippery hands. I will blame the Rat you pointed to cowering behind a chair. I blame the trembling of my hands as I grabbed that miserable broom to jab at him. I blame the blind surrender to fate that made me hurl the first blow knowing it was going to miss. I blame my blind fury, as I shoved around all the furniture, slinging the useless broom. I blame myself for letting it find its way to our room, where all would be lost. I blame myself for making it hide among our clothes, among these clothes. I lay all the blame on myself for letting you be a part of that grotesque hunt, you armed also with an old broom.

But most of all I stand accused of missing the killing blow, the one you finally struck to the pregnant Rat, because what's happening to us now would begin then, when I discovered myself naked, covered with goose pimples, a stick in my hand as if it were a spear and holding the dead Rat by the tail, looking at you, feeling myself looked at by your eyes glassy like the Rat's, out of whose snout trickled a string of blood.

Naín Nómez

was born in 1944, in Talca, Chile. He taught philosophy and Spanish American literature at the State Technical University and at the University of Chile until 1974. He now lives in Canada where he has published a bilingual book of his poetry, *Cuerpo de silencio*. He also edited and compiled the anthology *Literatura Chilena en Canada*. He has published poems, stories, and essays in Europe, Canada, and the United States.

ONDINA

A lo lejos, aún resonaban sus carcajadas cuando se hundió de nuevo en el lago. Me había visitado durante innumerables noches sin faltar ninguna y siempre dejaba en el aire los ecos de una risa ambígua que no podía comprender. Su cuerpo serpenteaba entre las rocas y las escamas de su piel brillaban a la luz de la luna como enjambres de luciérnagas. Desde el primer día sus ojos de gata en celo me cautivaron y cuando hundió su mano fría entre mis dedos, supe que me había atrapado en su urdimbre de besos y que volvería inevitablemente una y otra noche a regar con mi cuerpo sus profundidades marinas. Así aprendí secretamente a descifrar sus maniobras ardientes, mientras cavaba en sus profundidades como en una ciénaga helada. Las primeras estrellas nos sorprendían entramados furiosamente entre las algas y los lagartos gigantes rodando sin cesar de un lado a otro enceguecidos por la sombra que nos recortaba llenos de sangre y sudor, entre los cangrejos que nos clavaban sus pinzas y los lagartos que nos llenaban de lodo. Ella se dejaba beber como un agua putrefacta e inacabable, coleteando una y otra vez con sus escamas asperas que me mordían las piernas. Y de pronto comenzaba ese circular infinito entre la arena y las ondas barrosas de la orilla donde estrellas, cielo, luna, batracios viscosos y plantas rezumantes se juntaban en nuestra boca en un beso panteístico que terminaba al amanecer con la silueta de los caminos en las pestañas y un brillo carmesí en la piel que nos devolvía inevitablemente al placer recorrido.

Así nos acechamos por años. En las noches de tormenta nos guarecíamos en una caverna tapizada de helechos gigantes y rocas de amatista. Allí éramos como dos luceros con la luz desgastándose en ataques de frente y de costado hasta que nuestro amor se iba diluyendo en juegos y sueños que se rendían a la búsqueda monstruosa del

WATER NYMPH

From far off into the distance, her peals of laughter still resounded as she plunged once more into the lagoon. She had faithfully visited me every night for countless nights, leaving the echo of her subtle laughter hanging in the air, a laughter which I could never understand. Her serpentine body would slither down among the rocks and her scales would glitter in the moonlight like swarms of fireflies. From the first day that I saw her, her eyes like the eyes of a cat in heat caught me and when she pressed her cool hand into mine, I knew that I was trapped in her web of kisses and that she would inevitably return, night after night to water her oceany depths with my body. So I learned the secret art of decoding her burning movements as I plunged into her depths, like diving into an icy swamp. The first stars would surprise us, furiously entwined among the algae and the giant lizards, rolling languidly from side to side, blinded by the shadow that outlined us, covered with sweat and blood as the crabs snapped at us with their pincers and the lizards sloshed us all over with mud. She would let herself be drunk up like a rancid, bottomless pool, whipping her tail back and forth, its rough scales abraising my legs. Then suddenly she would start an endless, circular movement between the sand and the muddy waves of the shore where stars, sky, moon, clams, corals, and oozing plants would all come together into one long pantheistic kiss that would last until dawn with the silhouette of the roads against our eyelids and a crimson glow on our cheeks that inevitably reminded us of our recent pleasure.

And so we stalked each other for years. On stormy nights we took shelter in a cave hung with tapestries of giant ferns and amethyst rocks. There, we were like two morning stars, whose light was spent in fiery attacks from all directions, until our love at last became diluted into dreams and games that gave way to a monstrous search for the

minotauro. En los estíos ardientes proseguíamos nuestro placer de ébano en las aguas del lago cuyo efluvio nos volvía locos de alegría, compitiendo en cópulas abominables con las libélulas y los delfines como en el tercer día de la creación.

Pero sabía que ella irreconciliablemente tornaría a su orígen. Sus carcajadas eran cada vez más estridentes, sus cumbres de placer cada vez más desesperadas, sus mordiscos en mi piel ya lacerada cada vez más torturantes.

La última vez su cuerpo ardiente se pegó como un estuche de plata a mi cuerpo y su sal lúbrica y salobre me quemó las entrañas como un volcán de lava.

Cuando se fue, yo era como un pez moribundo varado en la playa. Su aliento ya casi fétido me quemaba los labios con un ardor entre nostálgico y asqueante. Su frío de metal había dejado un temblor en mis rodillas que aún hoy no logro evitar. Y en las pesadillas que recorren mis lóbregas noches, todavía sumido en el placer y el terror de su entrega, los escalofríos me sobreviven hasta la madrugada.

Al final me dijo: "Me he enamorado de un viejo tritón que me provoca los más deleznables apetitos. Tu pureza me corrompe." Ye se perdió con sus carcajadas azotando las aguas y derribando los árboles más cercanos.

Desde entonces la busco en los océanos más profundos y los puertos más tortuosos. Sé que tarde o temprano la encontraré prostituída en el mar de los Sargazos o derribada entre las mesas de una taberna por el viejo marinero de Coleridge. Sé que me reconocerá a pesar de mi pelo blanco y mis venas secas. Aunque me desprecie y me diga que estoy loco, me humillaré por tenerla en mis brazos. Enfrentaré a los asesinos del pueblo, la arrancaré de las manos de todos. Volveremos a vivir en la gruta de helechos y piedra, entre las algas secas y los minotauros hechos polvo. Y la crearé de nuevo con ese aire de ciénaga y llamas que me hizo perder la razón. Y la amaré con esa piel barrosa y húmeda que llevo adherida a mis escamas para siempre.

minotaur. In the burning summers we pursued our ebony pleasure in the waters of the lagoon whose invisible current drove us crazy with pleasure, as we competed with the dolphins and the dragonflies in abominable orgasms of joy, and it was like the third day of the Creation.

But I knew that she must inevitably return to where she had come from. Her peals of laughter were becoming more and more brittle, her peaks of pleasure more and more desperate, her bites into my lacerated skin more and more unbearable.

The last time her burning body adhered itself to mine, I felt locked, her body like a silver casket and her corrosive salt scalding into my entrails like lava.

When she went away, I was like a floundered fish left dying on the beach. Her rank breath still burned my lips with a half-nostalgic, half-disgusting ardor. Her metallic cold had left a trembling in my legs that still comes on me from time to time. In nightmares that recur through my gloomy nights, I am still submerged in the pleasure and the terror of surrender to her, and my whole body shakes until daybreak.

In the end, she told me, "I have fallen in love with an old merman who provokes the most animalistic desires in me. Your purity is corrupting me." And she was gone, in a peal of laughter, the force of it whipping the waters into a froth and uprooting all the nearby trees.

Since then I have searched for her in the deepest seas and at the bottom of the most treacherous ports. I know that sooner or later I will find her whoring in the waters of the Sargasso or thrown to the floor between the tables of some tavern, maybe by the Ancient Mariner. I know that she will recognize me in spite of my frosty hair and dried veins, and though she may think me mad, I will humble myself to have her in my arms again. I will face the murderers of the town, tear her from their hands and we will go back to live among the ferns in the cavern of stone, with the dried seaweed and the minotaurs. I will re-create her from the air of marsh and flames that drove me out of my head. I will love her with that muddy, wet skin that I wear clinging to my scales, forever.

149

Gonzalo Millán

was born in 1947 in Santiago, Chile. In 1968, he received the Pedro de Ona award for his book *Relación Personal*. In 1973, he went to Costa Rica on a scholarship from the Friedrich Ehert Foundation in West Germany. In 1974, he went to Canada, where he finished his M.A. at the University of Brunswick. He still lives in Canada and continues to publish his work there.

CORRESPONDENCIA

Del Sur dolorosamente lejos
vienen atados y quedos
a romper la rutina de aquí
que hiela y rutila.
En un camión llegan
y son descargados amigos
muertos en sacos de correo.

CARCEL

Me contó: Algunos
compañeros crecen
por entre las rejas
y a la calle salen
de alcantarilla
como helechos

MAIL

From the South, painfully far away
they come stealthily in bundles
to break the glittering frozen
monotony of this place.
They come on trucks
and are dumped dead
friends in mailbags.

PRISON

He told me:
some of the inmates
grow out through the bars
and into the street
they come up out of the sewers
like ferns

LA PAUSA

Se alejan como moscas caminando
por el cielo raso
y bajan el volumen
de la radio para escuchar
musica y no mis gritos
por un rato.

Pelan frutas y fuman
bromeando entre ellos
y conmigo
mientras cuelgo
de los pies cabeza abajo.

EL FUSILADO

A Raùl Barrientos

Frente al muro, arrodillado
bajo la manta espera su hora
mientras a su espalda
riendo unos soldados apuntan
a las suelas con ojos abiertos
de sus finales zapatos.

BREAKTIME

They move around like flies
crawling on the ceiling
they turn down the volume
of the radio so they can listen
to music instead of my screams
for awhile.

They peel oranges and smoke
telling jokes to each other
and joking with me
while I dangle
upside-down.

FIRING SQUAD

To Raùl Barrientos

Facing the wall, on his knees,
hunching under a blanket he waits his time
while behind him
laughing soldiers take aim
at the open eyes in the soles
of his last shoes.

Juan Camerón

was born in 1947 in Valparaíso. From 1972 to 1977 he lived in Buenos Aires. His works include *Las Manos Enlazadas*, 1971; *Una Vieja Joven Muerte*, 1972; *Perro de Circo*, 1979; and *Apuntes*, 1981.

UNA RAYA MAS AL TIGRE

Qué le hace el agua al pescado
al tigre una raya en el prontuario
al albatrós unas horas más de vuelo?
Pasarán camellos por agujas
poetas por puertas de juzgado
El tigre—ese poema con mil versos—
ese animal urbano—gruñe bajo suelo
lanza zarpazos a sí mismo
raya las paredes en silencio.

ONE MORE STRIPE TO THE TIGER

What does water mean to a fish
a stripe to the tiger in the eternal book
to the albatross a few more hours of flight?
Camels will pass through needles' eyes
poets through the portals of judgment
the tiger—poem of a thousand lines—
sublime animal—growls underground
swipes at its own shadow
stripes the walls of its tomb in silence.

Antonio Vieyra

was born in 1948. He is currently studying sociology. His major work is *Figura Inaugural,* a collection of poems.

Recorrer todo el camino
Buscando el amigo a quien se extraña.

Ver hombres obligados a curvarse.
Ver espejos diluyéndose en el tiempo.
Ver las palabras hundirse en el vacío.
Ver juntos a rencorosos, entusiastas,
              amigos, sabios y traidores,
              todos con la vista baja.

A fin uno se duerme
Lentamente.

Running down the same road all the way
Looking for the friend I've missed.

Seeing men forced to step out of the way.
Seeing mirrors fading into time.
Seeing words sink into the void.
Seeing misanthropes, enthusiasts, friends,
        wise men, traitors, and cowards all together,
        all with their eyes down.

Finally going to sleep
Slowly.

Inútil explorar la ciudad.
No se halla esquina alguna
Donde encontrar los sabios griegos.

Esperaré.

Quizás exista un minuto en el día,
Un indivisible minuto
Donde pasado y futuro se confundan.

Desnudemos el rostro.

No necesitamos un muro de palabras
ni de sombras
ni de sueños.

Crucemos el umbral de las rondas infantiles.

Useless to explore the city.
There is no ancient sage to be found now
Nor wise Greek in any place.

I will wait.

Perhaps there could be a minute in the day,
An indivisible moment
Where past and future are entangled.

————

Let us take off our masks.

We don't need a wall of words
of shadows
of dreams.

Let us cross over the threshold of childish rhymes.

Raúl Zurita

was born in 1951 and resides in Santiago. His poetry has appeared in numerous literary journals and in the anthology *Ganymedes 6*. His major works include *Purgatorio, Anteparaíso,* a bilingual edition of poetry (Anteparadise) and a critical work, *Literatura, Lenguage y Sociedad*. He is rapidly gaining stature as both a poet and literary critic. His poetry has been translated into English and German.

AREAS VERDES

NO EL INMENSO YACER DE LA VACA
bajo las estrellas su cabeza pasta sobre el
campo su cola silba en el aire sus mugidos
no alcanzan a cubrir las pampas de su silencio

GREEN AREAS

NOT THE IMMENSE GRAZING OF THE COW
beneath the stars nor her head a blob of dough
above the field her mooing nor the swishing of
her tail can ever fill the grasslands of her silence

Han visto extenderse esos pastos infinitos?

I. Han visto extenderse esos pastos infinitos
   donde las vacas huyendo desaparecen
   reunidas ingrávidas delante de ellos?

II. No hay domingos para la vaca:
    mugiendo despierta en un espacio vacío
    babeante gorda sobre esos pastos imaginarios

Have you seen how far those infinite fields extend?

I. Have you seen how far those infinite fields extend
    where the fleeing cows disappear into other pastures
    bunched up in weightless herds?

II. There are no holidays for the cow:
    awake and mooing in her vast void
    fat and driveling in those dreamy fields

Comprended las fúnebres manchas de la vaca
los vaqueros
lloran a frente a esos nichos

I. Esta vaca es una insoluble paradoja
    pernocta bajo las estrellas
    pero se alimenta de logos
    y sus manchas finitas son símbolos

II. Esa otra en cambio odia los colores:
    se fue a pastar a un tiempo
    donde el único color que existe es el negro

    Ahora los vaqueros no saben que hacer con esa vaca
    pues sus manchas no son otra cosa
    que la misma sombra de sus perseguidores

Interpret the mournful spots of the cow
the herdsmen
cry before those abysses

I. This cow is an unsolvable paradox
   she spends the night under the stars
   but she feeds on logos
   and her finite spots are symbols

II. That one though hates colors:
    she went to graze for a while
    where the only color was black

    Now the herdsmen don't know what to do with her
    her spots are nothing more
    than shadows of those who come to persecute her

Las había visto pastando en el radiante λογος?

I. Algunas vacas se perdieron en la lógica

II. Otras huyeron por un subespacio
   donde solamente existen biologías

III. Esas otras finalmente vienen vagando
   desde hace como un millón de años
   pero no podrán ser nunca vistas por sus vaqueros
   pues viven en las geometrías no euclideanas

Have you seen them grazing in the radiant λογος?

I. Some cows are lost in logic

II. Others have fled through a subspace
     where only biologies exist

III. Still others finally come wandering
      back from a million years
      but they can't be seen by the herdsmen
      they live in a non-euclidian geometry

Vamos al increíble acoso de la vaca
La muerte
no turba su mirada

I. Sus manchas finalmente
   van a perderse en otros mundos

II. Esa vaca muge pero morirá y su mugido será
    "Eli Eli/lamma sabacthani" para que el
    vaquero le de un lanzazo en el costado y esa
    lanza llegue al mas allá

III. Sabía Ud. que las manchas de esas vacas quedarán
     vacías y que los vaqueros estarán entonces en el otro
     mundo videntes laceando en esos hoyos malditos?

Let us follow the astounding life of the cow
Her look
is not altered by death

I. Her spots will finally
    be lost in another world

II. That cow moos but she will die and her mooing
    will be "Eli Eli/lamma sabacthani"
    so the herdsman will pierce her side and that thrust
    will go through to the great beyond

III. Did you know that the spots of those cows will
     remain empty forever and the herdsmen will be
     prophets in that other world lassoing in those accursed holes?

Sabía Ud. algo de las verdes áreas regidas?

Sabía Ud. algo de las verdes áreas regidas por los vaqueros y las blancas áreas no regidas que las vacas huyendo dejan compactas cerradas detrás de ellas?

I. Esa área verde regida se intersecta con la primera area no regida

II. Ese cruce de áreas verdes y blancas se intersecta con la segunda área blanca no regida

III. Las áreas verdes regidas y las blancas áreas no regidas se siguen intersectando hasta acabarse las áreas blancas no regidas

Sabía Ud. que ya sin áreas que intersecten comienzan a cruzarse todos los símbolos entre sí y que es Ud. ahora el área blanca que las vacas huyendo dejan a merced del área mas allá de Ud. verde regida por los mismos vaqueros locos?

Did you know about the green ruled areas?

Did you know about the green areas ruled
by the herdsmen and the white areas unruled
that fleeing cows leave squared off and closed behind them?

I. That green ruled area intersects
    with the first white unruled area

II. That crossing of green and white intersects
    with the second white unruled area

III. The green ruled areas and white unruled areas
     continue intersecting to the outermost boundaries
     of white

Did you know that now without intersections all symbols
begin to cross among themselves that now you are the
white area unruled which the fleeing cows leave
at the mercy of your great beyond which is green
ruled by those same crazy herdsmen?

Quién daría algo por esas auras manchadas?

Quién daría algo por esas auras manchadas que las
vacas mugiendo dejan libres en los blancos espacios
no regidos de la muerte de sus perseguidores?

I. La fuga de esas vacas es en la muerte no regida del
    vaquero Por eso no mugen y son simbólicas

II. Iluminadas en la muerte de sus perseguidores
     Agrupando símbolos

III. Retornando de esos blancos espacios no regidos
      a través de los blancos espacios de la muerte de Ud.
      que está loco al revés delante de ellas

Daría Ud. algo por esas azules auras que las vacas
mugiendo dejan libres cerradas y dónde Ud. está en
su propio mas allá muerto imaginario regresando de
esas persecuciones?

What would you give for those spotted puffs of air?

What would you give for those spotted puffs of air
that mooing cows leave free in the white space
where the deaths of their persecutors go unnoticed?

I. The flight of those cows in death is not ruled
    by herdsmen This is why they don't moo and are symbols

II. Glistening in the deaths of their persecutors
     Clustering symbols

III. Returning from those white unruled spaces
      from across the white space of your death
      which is crazy backwards before them

What would you yourself give for those blue puffs of air
which the mooing cows leave behind them free locked
where you in your own great beyond lie dead imaginary
returning from those persecutions?

EPILOGO

Hoy laceamos este animal imaginario
  que correteaba por el color blanco

EPILOGUE

Today we lasso this imaginary animal
   that rambled through the color white

Marjorie Agosín

was born in 1955. Presently teaching literature in Wellesley College, Massachusetts, she has published poems in journals, as well as critical works on the fiction of María Luisa Bombal and on the poetry of Neruda. Her two major books of poetry are *Hogueras* and *Brujas y algo más*.

FAMILIAS

Ardemos en la memoria
de todos los que han sido,
terror de salvajes incertidumbres,
amor de benignas hogueras.

Ardemos en una misma herida
o en el cuerpo dividido
que se une para
dislocarse en
un solo rostro
cubriendo
el rostro
que se besa.

Extendidas,
¿De quién son esas
piernas
que no las reconocemos
al ser arpegio
de un árbol,
de mil raíces
acariciando
cada longitud
de un
mismo cuerpo?

FAMILIES

We burn in the memory
of everyone that has been,
terror of incomprehensible savages,
love of warm hearths.

We burn in the same wound
or in the body divided
that joins again
to find itself
in a single face
covering
the face that kisses it.

Stretched out,
whose legs are those
that we don't recognize
as limbs
of a tree,
as a thousand roots
caressing
every line
of its own
body?

Armando Rubio

was born in 1955, the son of the well-known poet Alberto Rubio. His work has appeared in numerous journals, such as *Atenea* and *La Bicicleta*. His poetry also appeared in *Ganymedes 6*, the 1980 anthology of new Chilean poetry edited by David Turkeltaub. Armando Rubio was killed in December, 1980, when he fell from the sixth floor of a building.

LOS ESPEJOS

Los espejos roban la luz, los espejos
se tragan a los hombres
con enormes fauces centelleantes.

Los espejos se alimentan de secretos,
de oscuros desórdenes, de gestos.
Se puede viajar por los espejos,
visitar ciudades insondables,
entrar en ellos, robarles su secreto.

Los espejos
no tienen tiempo:
todos los espejos se llaman Moby Dick.

MIRRORS

Mirrors are thieves of light; they devour
men, swallowing them up
with greedy, shimmering gullets.

They feed on secrets,
on gestures, on dark confusions.
You can travel through the mirrors,
visit unimaginable cities,
enter the mirrors and steal their secrets from them.

Mirrors
have no concept of time;
all of them are called Moby Dick.

RENUNCIACION

No.
No iré al Paraíso.
La cuenta de la luz
me saldría muy cara,
y cara también el agua.

¿Y quién cocinará mis platos?
¿Esas radiantes cocineras
de blancos delantales
que caminan obedientes por el cielo?

No. Son demasiado caras también.
¿Y el teléfono?
A mí me gusta hacer llamadas
de larga distancia.
Me cortarían la comunicación
por pretencioso.

¿Y dónde voy a escribir?
No creo que tengan mesas
como la que hay en mi casa.
Además a mí me gustaría
estar siempre buscando a Dios.

No. Decididamente no.
El Paraíso es realmente caro.

RENUNCIATION

No.
I will not go to Heaven.
The electric bill
would be too expensive.
Also the water.

Who would fix my favorite foods?
Those radiant cooks
tripping around in their white aprons
obediently through the sky?

No. They're too expensive too.
And what about the telephone?
I like to make long distance calls.
They would probably
cut me off
just for spite.

And where am I going to write?
I'm sure they don't have desks
not like the one at my house.
Besides I prefer
to be always looking for God.

No. I'm afraid not.
Heaven is too expensive really.

The Fiction

Enrique Campos Menéndez

was born in Punta Arenas in 1914, a descendant of pioneer families. He has studied at universities in Salesiano, Buenos Aires, Madrid, and La Sorbonne. A screenplay writer and political journalist, he turned his attention to the writing of short fiction and finally, the novel. He has been Cultural Advisor to the Governor and General Director of Libraries, Archives and Museums. He is a member of numerous literary societies. He is best known now for his biographical novels and historical essays. A recent work, *Los Pioneros,* is a three-part non-fiction novel about the life of Magellan.

THE MISSIONARY

ON the day that the tall stranger came to the village of Oneisin, with his dry wisp of hair, his clear blue eyes, and short frizzle of a beard, enshrouded in a black cassock that came to his feet, the village *johon* realized that such an apparition would require all the arts of his office. So he approached the newcomer, while behind him trailed the brazen warriors, the frightened women, and the wonderstruck children, until they were all standing before the stranger waiting for their *johon* to speak.

The man took a few steps forward and pronounced a few friendly sentences in the language of the Onas. There was a rippling of surprise among the villagers. But the *johon* waved an imperious hand and proclaimed: "It is a man. A pale-faced man who speaks the language of our ancestors, and who says he possesses light."

The *johon* drew close to the stranger, so close he could feel the man's breath against his face. The villagers formed a tight circle around him. "Who are you?" the *johon* asked.

The stranger wrinkled his brow in a frown of perplexity. Then he spoke a strange word not in the Ona vocabulary: "Missionary."

"Mih-shaw-neh-ree," the *johon* repeated laboriously.

The mouths of the villagers palated the exotic word like a grape, making a slow, rhythmic refrain of its syllables, "Mih-shaw-neh-ree, Mih-shaw-neh-ree," chanting it over and over and finally dissolving into laughter.

Angrily, the *johon* silenced them. And the stranger began to explain his purpose in coming. He came from a far-off land, he said, bringing the message of God, the way to a better life, and the promise of eternal happiness.

The villagers shook with laughter. As they laughed, some of them even fell to the ground and rolled, so great was their merriment. But the *johon* put on a terrible scowl, which quieted the villagers, until they became very still, waiting to see what the *johon* would say and do next.

"Who is your God?" he asked, still standing next to the stranger.

"He who created the heavens and the earth, all men, animals, and plants, the only Lord and Master of all creation."

And now, undoubtedly, the villagers had something to laugh about. Even the *johon* himself could not refrain from making a gesture of scorn and disgust. Turning to the sea, he motioned with his hand toward the immense movement of the waves. Could anyone have created that? Was not that itself a god? The children turned their faces up to the sun, then back at the missionary, bobbing their heads innocently, which is the gesture of negation for the Onas. No—they seemed to say. *He* is the Father. The women looked anxiously for the pale white dish of the fading moon, which at that hour was still a tenuous tattoo on the skin of the sky. They pointed to its grave nocturnal solemnity, whispering, "Who could have created anything so beautiful?" The ancient ones, of course, they were the eternal ones who smiled down but restricted themselves from coming any closer than the most powerful mountain.

The *johon* summed up the expressions of all his villagers with a shrug of his shoulders and an angry crossing of his arms. A shadow of doubt clouded the brilliance of the eyes of the missionary, and his benign smile trembled a little. He closed his eyes and his beard began to move in a mysterious, whispering soliloquy.

"You will all come to an understanding," he said finally. There was a long silence. Besides his words, there was that voice, soft, deep, and passionate, that produced in them a strange influence.

"What is 'a better life?'" the *johon* then asked.

"A life of peace," responded the missionary. "That which flows from faith. That which sustains the earth. That which separates men from weapons, beasts, and birds. That which, if the enemy strikes you on the cheek, does not bring death but brings about the offering of the other cheek, disarming the enemy with forgiveness. . . ."

This time, the old ones seemed interested and their rugged yellow faces seemed to reflect the light in the eyes of the missionary. But the young ones looked incredulously down at the rigid earth, unbelievingly up at the trees petrified in the Fuegian landscape, their branches twisted and hostile, imagining for a moment what it would be like to let the wild goats and birds pass through those trees without sinking their arrows into their fleeing flesh, seeing themselves weak with hunger, trying to subsist on the meager pulp of the calafates root. Then, they looked to the distance, imagining other tribes coming against them with drums of war and they, running out to greet them weaponless, with open arms. At that moment, they felt the chilling shadow of the *Caranchos* demons and sensed the presence of death . . .

No, no it couldn't be. Wrathfully, they denied the evil news of the missionary.

Even the *johon* himself wondered if the stranger might have come to beguile them with that mysterious brilliance of his blue eyes and that sweet softness of his voice, tricks to deliver them into the hands of their enemies. He stroked his cheeks on which were tattooed the symbols of war. Also, he felt anger, but still there was a question to be asked and he controlled himself, betraying no more than an angry bob of his head.

"What is eternal happiness?" asked the *johon*.

The eyes of the missionary grew even more intense in their brilliance, became even steadier as he said, "*It's the life that continues after death.*"

These words produced a pregnant silence. Nobody moved. Everyone stared. The missionary sensed a rebirth of hope; a renewed power of persuasion filled his voice. "It's the happy life that waits for those who, having worshipped the True God and fulfilled his law, will live eternally after the death of the flesh. It's the life of joy, life without hunger, without pain, without hatred, in the heaven of my God."

And he explained what heaven was. His words, like paintbrushes, drew pictures before the astonished eyes of the Onas: of warm, luminous flower gardens, of trees hanging heavy with luscious fruit, where the women would always have before their eyes a shining lake in which to contemplate their loveliness, where the men would have bows, not to maim or kill with, only to please their ears with the melodious twang of their arrows. Where there would be neither old ones nor babies, for there in that place time did not exist, nor its wounds.

These and many other things the missionary told them, that day and for days after, until one day during one of his sermons, the *johon*, pressed by the unanimous sentiments of his followers, embraced the stranger. From that moment on, the Oneian code of hospitality was extended toward the missionary with the utmost extravagance. The *johon* felt obliged not to be jealous of this intrusion, though under other circumstances he would have thought of the stranger as a hated rival.

The young men and maidens, the ancient ones, and the children all began to conform, almost without realizing it, to the new way of life taught by the missionary, so they could have the right to the promised happiness. Each day they saw God, for each day the missionary would describe paradise and tell how it would be when they would one day meet God, when they would go to the place of the heavenly gardens carried on the wings of the words of the missionary.

Soon the desire for heaven had become an obsession for them. At all hours of the day they would beg for new and more complete descriptions. The missionary's accounts of heaven became even more lively, more and more full of images and yes—more sensual. Coming from a far-off land of merchants and poets, the missionary had acquired, in spite of himself, that precious gift of gab which persuades and enchants. And he accomplished a great deal. Too much even to hope for. The Onas began to practice his doctrine: first, since the idea of the one god was easy, much simpler than a hoard of gods to contend with, they accepted the one God, Lord and Master of all creation. Next, they began to meet the requirements to earn the "better life." They began to eat nothing but roots, nuts, and berries, leaving the birds, beasts, and fish in peace. And one day the *johon* told the missionary that if an enemy should enter their village, he would not only go to meet him with arms at his sides, he would offer him not only the other cheek, but his life as well.

The missionary, overcome with happiness, praised God for these wondrous manifestations.

Finally one day, which found them sitting and listening to the missionary's words as usual, weak and languid from a diet of roots and nuts, the *johon*, a light in his eyes much like that in the eyes of the missionary, jumped up and embraced him joyously, like someone about to begin a celebration.

"We've all resolved to die," he said, "to get to heaven soon! To be closer to God—close to our beloved God!"

The missionary, alarmed, started to interrupt him and explain about the terrible sin of suicide.

"No!" said the *johon,* without letting him speak. "We've resolved it.

And because we are so grateful to you, we give you this gift, not only because you lead us and guide us, but because you should be the first to taste eternal happiness."

With a pathetic smile that was almost a grimace, the missionary tried to hide his fear. Compelled to hold to his principles, at the same time determined to keep his life, his face reflected such a confused and ambiguous expression that the *johon,* misinterpreting it, said, "No, no, do not thank us. You have earned it."

He was perplexed. How could he beg for his life after having described the panorama of what comes after death? Besides, the missionary was—it must be understood—a true apostle and he was honor-bound neither to deceive nor to disillusion his converts. Nor could he say, like Paul among the heathen, "Lord, they have slain your prophets and destroyed your altars, and I alone remain faithful . . ."

For in Oneisin, they don't destroy God's altars. They raise them high, up to the very heavens.

And so they killed him.

Cecilia Casanova

is a well-known poet and short story writer. Among her books are *Los Juegos del Sol* (poems), *El Paraguas* (stories), and *De Acertijos y Premoniciones* (poems and stories).

THE UNMARRIAGE

To Eloise, it seems inexpressably unbearable. He hardly notices her all day, but when night comes, and it's time to turn out the light in the kids' room, she realizes, at the moment the darkness closes in around her, that she has cut off the only reason for communication between herself and Miguel. Now she can hear the sharp dripping of the leaky faucet in the bathroom; she'll have to remind him to call a plumber; after all, the house has to be kept going.

As happens every night, she is sitting on the edge of her bed when she hears Bernarda's voice from the hall: "Shall I serve dinner now?"

This is the worst hour for her, sitting across from Miguel. Sometimes he brings a book or a magazine. "Two strangers," she thinks. No. Worse than that. If a pair of strangers happened to be eating across from each other on a train, at least there would be a kind of bond between them, the little table swaying and the smiling steward standing over them, napkin folded over his arm. "Are you going to Valdivia? I hear it's raining pretty hard over there—I'm sorry! I didn't mean to bump you."

"Mental suicide," her friend Ellen had said. "Sooner or later it's going to end up in divorce."

More like later than sooner now. Eight years of her life, at least eight years it had been going on like this. Hard as she tried she couldn't focus on exactly how or when it had started. Probably it had been a slow process; when it's slow it hurts all the more. She would be grateful now if she could only hear him say, "Well, Eloise, between you and me it just . . ."

Better to let it play itself out.

The silverware barely touches the plates. Both try not to make any noise, and that makes the sounds around them seem louder. Eloise holds the water in her mouth, swallowing it in tiny gulps.

Later, at coffee, they get even with each other by stirring the coffee noisily in the cups. Eloise likes to scrape the sugar out of the cup until she can see the flower at the bottom of the porcelain, its paint cracked with age. This time, the coffee seems to have given it a different hue. The flower has become a measurement of time. When she sees it, she knows it's time to leave because there's nothing else to do. She'll tell him "Good night," as usual, but as her hand closes around the doorknob, she wonders if it wouldn't have been better to leave the room without saying anything.

José Donoso

was born in 1926 and is considered to be Chile's most prominent twentieth-century fiction writer. In his more than twelve books, which include novels, novelettes, and collections of short stories, his skill as a writer leads his readers into delightful worlds of the imagination, and so it is not surprising that he feels comfortable with the genre of poetry as well. His books, *El Obsceno pájaro de la noche, El Jardín de al lado,* and *El Lugar sin límites,* to name a few, are translated into English and other languages throughout Europe and the United States, as well as in South America.

SANTELICES

" 'Cause you've gotta understand, Santelices, that if we let all our
boarders do like you, we'd be in the poorhouse! Now we wouldn't
have denied you the right to nail a few nails, why you've lived at this
boardinghouse nearly three years and it looks like you'll be with us
permanently . . ." It was hard to imagine how Don Eusebio could talk
so much when the limp muscles of his toothless mouth seemed unable
to do anything but babble and pout. Santelices reflected that if he himself should give in to the temptation not to wear his false teeth, as
Bertha suggested—"Feel free, Santelices, feel free," she'd tell him. "Be
comfortable, be at home. There are no pretty girls to impress around
here."—then in a short time his mouth would be looking just like that.
"But to nail twenty-five nail holes is just too much!"

"Twenty-three," Santelices stammered.

"Twenty-five, twenty-three, what's the difference! Put yourself in
my place. What would the wallpaper look like in this house if everybody took it into his head to nail twenty-five posters on the wall? Do
you realize? After that, who'd want to rent the rooms? You know how
finicky some people are, and critical, when they come to rent a place. I
bet before you came here, you didn't know the meaning of the word
'privilege.'"

"Yes, but they weren't nails, they were . . ."

"Tacks, nails, what's the difference? Look at that wall. And that
other one. I don't know what my daughter Bertha's going to say when
she sees it. And how much's it gonna cost me to repaper it all? Think
about that! And those paper hangers, what they charge these days, the
sons of bitches!"

"But the paper was old . . ."

"Do me a favor, Santelices. Tell me whatever demon possessed you
to tack up all those hideous animal pictures anyway? And where in
God's name did you get so *many*? Frankly, I find it a little strange. Like
something a crazy person would do. And the last thing in the world

I'd call you is crazy, Santelices. Why I was telling Bertha the other day that if all our boarders were like you, so courteous and good-mannered and neat with their things, this business would be a pleasure to run instead of the drudge that it really is . . ."

"Thank you very much, but I . . ."

"You don't have to thank me. It's the pure truth. Besides, you're like part of the family, almost a relative, so to speak, above all 'cause you're so easy-going, not pretentious like some. And I'll tell you something private, man to man, don't repeat it around here, but . . . my daughter Bertha, well . . . you know, she . . ."

"The very idea, Don Eusebio!"

The old man lowered his voice. "Now if these posters were pin-ups, naked women for instance, or girls in little black g-strings or something, I'd understand it. What can I say, I'd understand it. I'm an old man, but you know me, and you know I'm young at heart, so to speak. And I wouldn't say a word to Bertha. But this . . . this is a bit strange, Santelices, you can't tell me it ain't."

"I don't know about that but . . ."

"And look how it leaves the wallpaper! Look at that hole!"

"But Don Eusebio, if I'm going to be keeping the room anyway . . ."

"And look at this one! The plaster behind it is falling down onto the sheets! And I changed those sheets myself just last week! My God! Before my poor daughter has a heart attack I've got to call the paper hangers and get an estimate, and whatever it costs, you'll have to pay for it, that's all there is to it."

So Don Eusebio left, clutching a fistful of crumpled posters to prove to Bertha how perverse their boarder was.

II

Santelices was late for work that morning.

Usually, he would put on his socks and underwear sitting on the edge of the bed. On cold mornings, he would dress under the covers, warmed by the body heat trapped under the blankets. Now it was two minutes before 8:30, which was the time he should be there. Sitting on the edge of the bed, he hesitated, not knowing what to do. His beautiful posters that he had so meticulously tacked all over the walls were in total disarray from the intrusion of Don Eusebio—some were wrinkled and torn, some were lying in the floor, some were tangled with the bedclothes and the pajamas, mingled with the smell of his own body.

Going up to his room the night before, after playing canasta, Santelices had already known what he was going to do . . . the secret longing had been growing within him for a long time now, and passing in front of a hardware store a few days ago, he'd bought two pounds of tacks. It had been extremely difficult to sleep after that, feeling those long, yellow eyes, those padded paws, those sinuous bodies filled with the lethargic heat of other climates, trapped like prisoners in the bottom of his dresser. It was as if he could hear them howling, and he couldn't resist, in spite of the fact that it was nearly three in the morning.

For last night, as if Bertha had guessed that after he went up to his room he was going to engage in something that did not include her, she'd kept the canasta going hand after hand, to an unbelievable hour. Santelices was sleepy and had protested that he had to get up early the next day to go to work. And besides being sleepy he was burning with the desire to go up to his room—as on other nights when Bertha had been more reasonable about the time—to pore over his portfolios of photos, clippings, and sketches; his scrapbooks and albums; his manilla envelopes full of drawings clipped from magazines, articles, and picture books. Since Bertha had discovered how addicted he was to their nightly rounds of canasta with her father and a dead person, she, knowing that Santelices would never leave while there were cards on the table, could easily prolong the game as long as she wanted.

They never played for money. Each one had his little bag of beans: fat, shiny white beans that looked as if they were made of porcelain—these took the place of money. On Saturdays they counted up. The loser would take the others out to the movie of their choice. Then, she'd put all the beans back and they'd start over.

Near the end of the round, Santelices was almost asleep. The cards were heavy in his hand; his eyelids were fluttering until the table—the whole dining room—had become a huge salad of hearts, clubs, diamonds, and spades. At each turn, Bertha would give him a sharp nudge.

"Okay, Santelices. Your turn. The good thing about canasta is it's supposed to move fast, especially if you're playing with a dead person."

"Tonight we might as well be playing with two dead ones," muttered Don Eusebio, and gave such a cackle of laughter that Santelices felt his dental plate rattle.

"That's enough, Father," Bertha rebuked him. "You act more like eight years old than eighty. Don't laugh so loud."

Finally, Santelices revived when Don Eusebio began to invent new rules for the game in his own favor. At first, Santelices just let it pass; he was so tired he didn't want to argue, and his only desire was for the game to be over. But he could take it no longer when Don Eusebio asserted that for canasta to be played right, the player could take the deck with a card and a wild card before going down, if that other card were an ace. Indignation woke Santelices as if he had been hit.

"You can't do that," he said loudly, grabbing the old man's hand which was already extended toward the deck.

Bertha choked on the grenadine she'd been drinking.

"Are you accusing my father of cheating?" she asked.

"You can't, you can't." Santelices' voice rose shrilly. "When I was vacationing in the hot springs at Panimávida, I met a woman from Uruguay . . ."

"When did you ever vacation at the hot springs?" shouted the old man, his hand still a prisoner in Santelices' grip.

"Let go of my father, for pity's sake. Don't be ridiculous," said Bertha. "And you know I hate liars."

"On top of that, he accuses *me* of lying," whined Don Eusebio. "Give me a drop of that grenadine, honey, all this excitement's made me thirsty for something sweet."

"No. I don't have much left."

"You'll get bloated on it! Half a bottle's too much for you in one night!"

"You can't pick up the deck," insisted Santelices. "You can't, you can't. Nobody cheats me like that."

"Who's gonna cheat over a few lousy beans?" grumbled Don Eusebio.

"And the movie? You call that nothing? For the past four Sundays I've been taking you two out!"

"Bah, the movie, the movie."

"This canasta game is a drag," said Bertha. "I've never been so bored in my life. So let's finish it. Majority wins. What do you say, Santelices? Can you or can't you pick up the deck with an ace and a wild card before going down?"

"You can't."

"You can't, one vote. Well, I vote you can. One vote for and one against. Father. Can you or can't you?"

"You can't," said the old man, distracted from staring hungrily at the bottle of grenadine.

Bertha, indignant at her father's confusion, which she said made her look like a fool, grabbed up all the cards, slapped them together in a heap on the table and stood up. She left without saying good night, leaving the men to pick up the cards and put them away. She did not forget, though, to take her little bag of beans.

Climbing the stairs to his room, drunk with drowsiness, Santelices was thinking he had only a few hours left until time to get up and leave for the office. Through a broken glass in the skylight, a steady leak was dripping into a washpan. From the rooms along the dark hallway, he could hear the deep snores of the other boarders, with whom Bertha and Don Eusebio never associated, bestowing this favor on him alone. The cold, sharp feel of the key in his hand and the rasp of metal in the keyhole aroused him slightly. The key still in his hand, he put on his pajamas and then crouched before the dresser and opened the bottom drawer.

He had only to dump the large envelopes onto the bed and spread their contents over the room and everything would be transformed. New odors, powerful and animal, permeated the air, overcoming the ordinary smells of daily life. Huge branches and strange foliage sprang up, ready to tremble after the quick leap of a heavy body, and in the depths of the vegetation, the bushes crackled beneath the weight of a stealthy paw as the tall grass parted with sinewy figures that marauded through it. The air was putrid with animal breath; the green-violet shade and the blotchy light moved together with the menacing presence of power and grace, of life-threatening beauty lying in wait.

Santelices smiled. This, Bertha was incapable of understanding. Nothing mattered now—sleep, the lateness of the hour, Bertha, the office—time had extended itself in a gracious and generous embrace. Santelices took out all of them. He draped them over the bed, the floor, the table, the dresser, the bureau. He gazed at them lovingly and at great length. Then he got out his two pounds of tacks. His collection was the greatest, the most beautiful in all the world. Better be-

215

cause he'd never talked of it to anyone or showed it; this secret security was all he needed to make him feel superior, strong, proud, able to face them all, and to know that no one would ever guess where his inner strength came from and what he kept locked in the bottom drawer of his dresser.

Years ago, with his first paycheck from his salary as a librarian, he'd celebrated by treating himself to a box of chocolates tied with a blue ribbon. On the box cover was a picture of a beautiful feline, the domestic type, playing with a ball of yarn. After the candy was all gone, he couldn't bear to throw away the box, it was so beautiful, so he'd kept it for years and years.

Sometimes he'd think about that little smile that wasn't a smile exactly, and the hint of danger in that little paw raised to show tiny claws half-hidden. Then he'd take out the box and stare at it for a long time. The obsession grew until he wanted something more; it wasn't enough. His impulse to keep the box was overtaken by a new longing; what he'd seen in it was diluted and the feeling was totally absent now.

One afternoon as he was thumbing through some old magazines in a used book store, he discovered a documentary with colored photographs of felines, not the domestic type, but those that live in the jungle and kill. He remembered his cat on the chocolate box, and his new-found love wiped out the old as he gazed fondly. Here in these pictures, he had it all: naked cruelty, the threat of danger—they seemed to accent the beauty, to endow it with crouching grace, to bring it to the boiling point, the flaming point, the blinding point, leaving him with sweaty palms and pounding heart. Delighted with what he'd found, he bought the magazine. From then on, in his time off, he'd browse through the bookstores, looking for something, anything, that would prolong this feeling, heighten it, amplify it. He bought everything he could find. Sometimes, he was tempted by expensive books that would leave him broke for weeks. Sometimes he'd even buy foreign ones, written in languages he could not read, just to be able to leaf through them, caressing the pages, as if they could give him that something, that something he was looking for.

Months would go by in which he'd find nothing. In the half-light of his room, beneath the soft blue globe of his table lamp, he'd gaze at the posters, searching for that straying passion among them, and they would seem disappointingly un-alive, reduced to paper and ink, and something within him too was un-alive. The depth of his search would heighten his imagination, producing within him such a blinding and paralyzing tangle that there was no room for anything else.

It was one of those afternoons that Bertha had said to him as he came down the stairs, "Hey, Santelices, what's going on up there that makes you come down so pale and crazy-looking?"

It was as if she had invaded that small private part of him that was all he had left.

One day he'd left the office early, claiming to be sick, and he'd gone to the zoo. He'd spent a long time gazing into the cages of the big cats. The flies buzzed around their heads and gathered on their rotting excrement. Their tails were filthy, their coats mangy and lustreless. The cages were disappointingly small. When the keepers came to throw them slabs of meat on long hooked sticks, the beasts threw themselves onto the bloody scraps of flesh and gulped them down with growls and smacking noises, crunching the bones and slobbering hungrily. Santelices left in a hurry. It was something of what he was looking for, but not that exactly. For in all his hours of perusing the bookstores and staring at the cages in the zoo, nothing could compare with those first beautiful prints he'd found where the jungle cats, with their triangular smiles gleaming, prowled across the pages with a stealthy stance like the fulfilling insinuation of death itself. Hungrily, he began looking for the ferocious scenes, with the steaming throats still fresh with the heat of their victims' blood, or scenes in which the great cat's body was coming down over its bloody, powerless prey. Santelices' heart pounded in his chest with the heart of the victim, and to save himself, he would fix his eyes on the killer, the better to identify with him.

So, the night before, he had released to freedom the most beautiful ones, his princes, his favorites. He had tacked them above the headboard of his bed, near the bureau, and above the wardrobe, where they'd be in full view. Then he'd stretched out on the bed and stared at them for a long time, feeling them take over the room. He could hear the menacing sounds, which could only be their growling or the snap of a tree branch beneath their heavy paws. He could see in the semi-darkness the quick raising of pointed ears, bodies moving, eyes blinking which seemed to be glowing with fire; smell the odors, whiffs of pungent air breathed in and out of powerful lungs; feel their presence scraping the room, the heat of their glossy coats stretched tautly over the sinewy limbs, elegant graceful muscles, and everything a blood-tingling invitation to participate in the red-hot, savage life, to lay oneself open to the way of blood and gullet, prey and predator.

Then Santelices had fallen asleep.

It was less than an hour later when Don Eusebio had knocked on the door, coming in without waiting for an answer. Turning on the light, he had come to ask the favor that Santelices certainly wouldn't mind: that he should get up earlier than usual because the hot water heater in one of the bathrooms was broken and it would help a lot if there were fewer people trying to use the other one during the time that most of them were getting ready for work. He never finished what he was going to say, for it was then that he saw all the posters on the wall, and he was speechless, his toothless mouth open with amazement. A second or two later, he started into his tirade about the walls and demanded that Santelices tear those things down immediately.

After the old man left, Santelices took a long time to get dressed. He didn't care about being late for work, he'd been working at that office for sixteen years and it had never happened before. At last he stood up, and as he tiptoed downstairs, his stomach was churning with the dread that Bertha would hear him leave. He turned around on the stairs and went back to his room to change to some soft-soled shoes. He started back down, more quietly than ever before. Had he left the light on in his room? As softly as he could, he slipped toward the door, but still there came the shout he had expected to hear.

"Santelices?"

He stopped, hat in the air over his bald head. "Did you call me, Bertha?"

"Don't be smart with me. Come here."

Before entering her room, he hesitated, his hand on the doorknob, and stared at two dead flies, dried up many years ago no doubt, pressed between the dusty window curtain and the glass. Bertha was still in bed, sunk down in what looked like a sea of fat pillows on the huge, queen-sized bed.

The nightstand was cluttered with things: a box of talcum powder, a brush with hair sticking in it, combs, bobby pins, curlers, and perfume bottles. Near the bed stood Don Eusebio like a sentinel with a broom in his hand and dust cloth tied around his head.

"Have you nothing better to do than stand around here like an idiot?" Bertha snapped at him. And the old man fled, muttering something about having to fill in for the maid she'd fired two weeks ago.

When they were alone, Bertha lowered her eyes and began to sob softly. Her hands trembled on the blue velvet coverlet. Her immense bosom puffed up and down like a huge balloon that inflated and deflated. The tears rolled down her fat, powdered cheeks. Seeing her, Santelices guessed that Bertha had planned this whole thing just for him, and he had an overwhelming urge to get out.

"Santelices!" he heard again. He was imprisoned in her gaze, now dry-eyed.

"Well, uh . . ."

"Come on, speak up!"

"Well, I'd like to say that if I . . ."

"How is it possible after all I've done for you?" She started to cry again. "All those horrible pictures. How you must hate me."

"How can you say that?"

"Yes, yes, you hate me . . . and after I've acted just like a mother to you, taking care of you after that operation, fixing you all those special foods, staying up beside your bed so you wouldn't be lonely, and I even let you use my room, my very own bed so you would be comfortable and get well sooner. I think you're the most ungrateful person I've ever met!"

With a cold chill, Santelices remembered his convalescence in Bertha's room, after the operation for his ulcer. He'd expected the month of paid sick leave to be a paradise vacation, all that time to himself to peruse his albums and daydream in the quiet repose of his room! All that time to read and learn, about their strange ways and habitats, and the distribution of the species. But before he could even protest, Bertha had installed him in her own room downstairs. While he was still too weak to resist, he was moved in there where she could keep watch over him day and night, and she spent the whole time hovering over him, boring him with her problems, choking him with her presence, not giving him a minute to himself. She entertained him, she stayed up with him, and read into his every word and gesture a desire that wasn't there, a request for something he didn't really want. And all the while, up there in his own room, those eyes glowed blindly in the darkness, those perfect bodies remained flat in the drawer of his dresser, trapped in there the entire month. For Bertha wouldn't hear of his climbing the stairs for anything until she was perfectly satisfied that he had been nursed back to health.

"But I did appreciate it, Bertha."

"Did you really?" she asked. She had suddenly stopped crying. She picked up a handful of the pictures Don Eusebio had brought down. "You appreciated it, did you? And you think that gives you the right to destroy the room you live in anytime you want? And those *horrible, nasty* pictures! That's why you've been shutting yourself up in your room! I know all about how you people are! And you're not going to be doing any more weird things in this house unless I know about it; we don't let things like that go on in our house! We might be poor folks, but we're *decent* people. Who does he think he is?" she asked the walls. "Who does he think he is to walk in here and filthy up our house so decent people won't want to live here." She turned back to him. "You want the fig peeled and put in your mouth, that's what you want! Just like all men, thinking some dumb woman like me is going to work and sacrifice and after that you can do weird, nasty things and not tell her . . . and after that you hate her!"

"The very idea, Bertha. You know I'm very fond of you."

"Don't mock me just because I'm a poor spinster and have to take care of my aging father, a feeble old man who's not even strong enough to defend me! You know him now as he is, but in his younger days, you should have seen him. How he made us suffer, my God. A tyrant, like all men, selfish, mean, and nasty—just like you, look at those pictures, you can't deny it, the only way to describe them is *nasty!* And all that time, playing canasta like a saint, so you could go tomcatting around . . . why not? You think I'm a fool. I'm going to clean up that room and put fresh new wallpaper in there, the most expensive I can find and after that you're going to pay for it no matter how much it costs. As soon as you leave I'm going up there, and if I catch a cold from being out of bed it'll be *your fault!*"

Seeing the huge body of Bertha rising toward him from the satin sheets and the tumble of pillows, indecently clad in a see-through nightgown she had bought from a woman who had bought it on the black market on vacation, Santelices fled. The stuffy smell of the airless room, mixed with the scent of talcum powder, rosewater, and grenadine, and the odor of the body of an old virgin followed him down the corridor and the four blocks to his office. He climbed the five flights of stairs two at a time, the elevator being out of order, and went in without saying hello to anyone and shut himself up in his office, asking not to be disturbed and to hold all his business until Monday; it being Friday, he had a lot of catching up to do. He paced up and down beside the loaded bookshelves. He would sit down at his desk and get back up again. He stared at some pigeons pecking on the sill outside his office window. From time to time, they'd stop and look up at him. From the window he could see down to the narrow patio, a sunroof cut in half by shadow and beams of light, with the clouds crossing the sky. Down on the sunroof a slim, blonde girl was playing with a cat, five floors below him. He tried not to think about anything, tried to push away the thought of going home to that house which he knew now had nothing for him.

After leaving the office that day, Santelices went for a walk through the streets of the city, and wandered down to the zoo, closed to the public at this hour. Taking a turn and then another around the outskirts of the park walls, he finally stopped, recognizing among all the animal smells the familiar one. From the prisons of the cages he could hear faint roars that gradually trailed off, fading out in the evening air. His only desire now was to hear nothing, see nothing, so he left as the night suddenly closed in around him, and he kept on walking aimlessly through the streets. He stopped and had a sandwich; it was too spicy and he thought about his ulcer. Then he went to a 3-D movie and fell asleep in the balcony. When he came out it was one o'clock in the morning. Surely at Bertha's boardinghouse there would be nobody up at this hour. So he decided to go back.

In the corridor there was an odor of burnt paper, overlying the smell of fried fish—that every-Friday-smell that never seemed to completely go away. Besides all this, there was a heavy silence about the place, as if nobody lived there.

He spent some time looking all over his room for his posters, and scrapbooks, his albums and Manila envelopes full of clippings; he looked under the bed, in the drawers, on top of the wardrobe. Finally he got cold and went to bed, reluctantly, after making a few more feeble searches, but with the resignation that it was useless. He knew; he'd been sure even before he'd left the office that Bertha had taken everything. She must have burned them. All day at the office he'd rehearsed in his mind how he would take his leave of them. What else could he do? Reconciliation was impossible. Forgiveness was out of the question. He envisioned himself standing in front of Bertha like a little boy, asking for her to give back what belonged to him. He imagined her there touching them, turning the pages before his eyes without letting him have them; it destroyed the beauty of their existence. The very thought of her having been near his magnificent beasts, the idea of her hands on them was enough to pop the bubble of enchantment that surrounded them. They were defiled, reduced to nothing more than purchases, books of different sizes and weights, two-dimensional drawings on paper, and colored inks. The sublimity of the great cats could never be rescued. It was as if Santelices had burned them himself one by one in a huge bonfire that was now extinguishing, ever so slowly.

He started the habit of getting up at dawn to avoid Bertha and Don Eusebio. He would come back very late, exhausted, and throw himself onto the bed, letting the heavy dreamless sleep take over his consciousness. He lived on sandwiches, peanuts, caramels, until his digestion, which had always been delicate, began to give way. At the office, no one noticed anything; he was always neat, courteous, and obliging. Since it was a slow period, he had extra time to just sit and do nothing. He would stare out the window at the sky, give crumbs to the pigeons that perched on the sill, and stare at the activity on the patios below him, especially the slim blonde girl who always seemed to be out there on the sunroof five floors down. She was always busy at something: washing clothes, arranging and trimming the plants, playing with the cat, or brushing her long, thick blonde hair.

Sometimes in his afternoon walks he'd pass houses with signs that said, "Rooms to Let." He'd go in and look around, calculate moving costs, living expenses, chat with the landlady, who'd always be delighted at the possibility of such a respectable pensioner. Santelices always ended the interview finding some defect or other, the light in the bathroom, the stairway too inconvenient, the bedroom ceiling cracked, but these were all just excuses. He couldn't fool himself. He realized he would never be able to leave Bertha's boardinghouse. It was too hard to start over and build a new relationship with someone, and the thought was painful to him, leaving him with the definite ache of apprehension. At his age, he realized that if he wanted comfort, it was going to cost him. Where else could he go and feel accepted, just knowing that he had a place to play canasta every night without his false teeth in, and that his shirt would never lack a button, his shoes would always be polished in the mornings, and the irregularities of his stomach would be humored, as would his likes, his few dislikes; all this was worth something. It'd be a shame to have to leave all that. Still, he could not yet bring himself to come back to the house at an hour when he'd be obliged to face Bertha and take a definite stand about his lost posters and albums. It was true he'd committed an infraction in regard to the wall. They'd had the right to take them down. But each time he thought about it, he felt a hot, searing pain in the gut . . . they'd burned them; he was sure of it. But he'd rather do anything than humiliate himself by a confrontation with Bertha. He could not put out his hand and ask for them. But after awhile, the longing to return to custom, to pick up again the canon of existence of the former order in his life took over, even though he could not put into words what it was that was missing. He pondered these things every day as he went over and over what he would do about it, standing by the window of his office looking out. In the window across the street was a new sign that said "Leiva Brothers." Who in the world could they be, and five floors below him, on the patio of the sunroof, the girl was sewing. It was a pity he could not see her face. She must be extraordinarily beautiful, playing there with the pussycat. He knew it was a female because now there were kittens, five, maybe six of them, and the little creatures cavorted around the girl, and she would play with them and feed them milk from a saucer.

Perhaps it was magic that had produced the kittens and made him forget his fears. For one afternoon, he went straight back to the house after work, as if nothing had ever happened, and with the intention of assuming a natural demeanor that would erase all ill will on his part, leaving the burden on Bertha. There had never been, he had to admit, any disagreeable incidents between them until now. But be that as it may, they would have to learn to get along sooner or later, so they may as well get this out of the way, get it over with before his stomach should totally disintegrate and his feet wear out from all that walking around the streets at night.

He went into the house whistling. He saw that Bertha had heard him, for she quickly turned off the water in the bathroom and stepped out as he was coming toward the stairs, as if they would see each other by accident. Santelices went on as if he hadn't seen her, then from the landing, he turned and glanced down where she was standing, staring up at him, drying her arms with a towel.

"Oh, Bertha," he said. "Good afternoon." Then he went on up without hearing whatever it was she would say. When he got up to his room, he stretched out on the bed, smiling.

Suddenly the emptiness seemed quite pleasurable to him, spacious, though a little dark, a new life without even the threat of printed paper, without the torturous invitation he would extend to himself day after day, night after night, for so many years, without really being in life, except to participate in the far-off echoes of its existence.

He dozed a little while until he heard a soft knock at the door. "Santelices?"

"Bertha? Come in, come in."

Santelices could feel Bertha's hand leaving the doorknob at his invitation. "No, no thank you. You must have many things to do."

He didn't answer and waited to see what she would do next. After a few seconds, she continued. "I just came up to tell you that supper will be ready in a quarter of an hour, that is if . . ." There was a tentative pause, a silence which he did not fill. "I made that chicken dish you liked so well . . ."

"Which one? I don't remember," he answered.

He could feel again Bertha's hand on the doorknob, hesitantly, as she went on, "That recipe we found in that Argentine magazine, do you remember? And I tried it out for my father's birthday . . ."

"Oh, yes, well . . . I'll come down in a while."

"Great, then, but there's no hurry . . . it'll be ready in a quarter of an hour."

Bertha seemed to remain at the door for a minute, no, for just a few seconds more than necessary before going back through the corridor, humming a tune. He stayed like that for a while, then got up, splashed some water on his face at the lavatory, combed his hair, straightened his tie, and went down.

The chicken was delicious. Santelices had to admit that Bertha was an excellent cook. She could do anything in the kitchen when she condescended to. She seemed to be drowning in his flattery. You have the hand of an angel, Bertha. The hand of angel. It'll be a happy man that spends his life with you. She served him three helpings.

They turned on the radio to hear "Nights in Spain," the nighttime drama that Don Eusebio liked so well, listening with a suspicious overenthusiasm, as if obeying some secret plan. Bertha kept looking at her father severely, and when he started telling his usual dirty jokes, she cut him off and proposed a game of canasta. They all agreed brightly, and Bertha got out the deck. The hands went quickly, smoothly, hands up, hands down. Santelices won one hand after another without even a protest from Bertha or the old man.

"Wow, look how full your beanbag is now, Santelices. You're getting rich on us, eh?"

"Will you put it away for me, please?"

"Yes, of course."

At the end of the week, Santelices' bag was heavy and theirs were thin. Don Eusebio was a little piqued at having to pay for the movie that Sunday, and he didn't say much. He buried his nose in the racing section of the paper until Bertha jerked it away from him. Finally, Santelices chose *Volcano of Passion* for Bertha, for she'd been talking about wanting to see it. She'd heard about it from that woman she'd bought the nightgown from—the movie was all about a beautiful woman whom everyone thought was wicked, but who actually was a wonderful person. They were both so nice to Santelices that week, that finally he got up enough courage to ask Don Eusebio to loan him his binoculars. The old man hadn't used them since he'd left off going to the races, after many arguments with Bertha, and tears and chidings, until he'd given up the vice.

Santelices explained that he wanted them to pass the time from the window of his office, since they were in a slow time right now, and he could use them to amuse himself looking out of his window there at work. He didn't go into detail about it, but all he really wanted to do was gaze at the girl who played with her kittens all day, every day, on the sunroof below him.

When he got to the office, he went directly to the window, but he had a hard time getting the binoculars into focus right off. His anxiety to get it perfect caused his fingers to be clumsy, and he kept thinking he could still get a better focus and it wasn't quite good enough. But at last he was satisfied.

He could see now that she was about seventeen, delicate, with that thick, blonde hair, and such a sad, melancholy look about her that seemed to say she belonged to no one and to nothing. Santelices was beside himself. All around her frolicked the little kittens, eight, maybe nine of them, calicoes, tiger ones, Persians, all babies of the enormous cat that was sleeping in her lap. Santelices felt his heart skip a beat at the unusual size of the mother cat. He scanned the patio with his binoculars. Wasn't that another huge cat crouching in the shade by the washtub? And what were those shadows moving behind the plants?

As the afternoon went on, Santelices could see that, from the top of the half-wall of adobe that surrounded the patio, and creeping along the window embrasure, and sliding down from a tree he hadn't noticed before, more cats were coming down to the patio, and the girl was caressing them, smiling. What went on in that patio after dark when all the offices of this building were closed? It's well-known that felines become different creatures at night, that something changes them, filling them with a ferocity that is not there in the daytime. Was that girl going to stay out there all night with those indolent beasts?

As he continued to bask in the special attention they were still pouring on him there at the house, it was easy to forget the excitement aroused by the girl. Still, it would be his secret, and if ever the courtesies of Bertha should start to wear off, as he dreaded each day they might, he still had the consolation of a friendship from afar with the slender blonde girl who lived in the apartment with the sunroof. This thought brought him so much security that one day he grew bold enough to say to Bertha, when he knew she was serving hash for supper, "I don't like hash, I want chicken."

"Chicken two times in one week, and not even out of his own pocket—will you listen at that!"

"Yes, well, I just feel like having chicken."

Then Bertha lost her temper. "Now see here, Santelices. That's really stepping over the line—and all because you know that you . . . that we . . ."

Something was showing in Bertha's eyes now, which after all these weeks was blatantly obvious. As she spoke, she was rolling up the sleeves of her flowered housecoat, looking at him without blinking, and pouring herself a tall glass of grenadine. Santelices spoke quickly, before her look could banish his boldness, "Say, Bertha, tell me something. Do you remember those pictures of mine, those posters I put on my wall a while back and later I couldn't find them? Would you happen to know whatever became of them?"

Bertha almost dropped her glass of grenadine. The hard look in her eyes dissolved before Santelices' innocent gaze.

"My God, Santelices, how you complain about your old pictures! What do you mean by bringing that up now, after almost two months? Aren't you ashamed of going around playing games like a child! After all that . . . well, after *that,* I was talking with my father and we decided that since you were probably thinking of keeping the room . . ."

"Yes, well, maybe," he interrupted.

Bertha's eyes fixed on his and never left them as she went on, "So we decided that it wasn't worth it to repaper or to charge you anything. You don't have to worry about it."

"Well, that's certainly kind of both of you."

He waited for her sigh of relief. Then he went on, "But, my posters?"

"Oh, that. Well, my God, Santelices. I wish you'd stop being so silly. How should I know what became of them? Didn't I tell you I gave them to Father? Why don't you go ask him about it. Of course, there's just one thing, I . . . don't know what you'll think about this, but . . . I thought I'd keep one of the big colored prints; I framed it in that big blue frame from the mirror that the tenant in number 8 left behind. If you want to see it, it's hanging in my room, and you can come by and look at it sometime . . . it's a real beauty—and I know the name of the animal, such a lovely creature, there among all those rare, exotic plants . . . I saw a movie once where . . ."

Santelices left without saying anything.

The next day, Santelices stayed in the office until everyone was gone. As soon as night was falling, in that wing of the alley across from him, all the lights of all the offices were going out one by one, until the giant concrete building had acquired a totally new essence all its own, that of a huge, empty cement box. A breath of air, pregnant with expectation, came wafting in the open window. He was alone with the girl among the cats five floors below. The shadows sank, falling block by block in the tiny patio, lit up only by the fire of yellow eyes, green eyes, red eyes, blinking. Santelices could barely make out the forms, even with the help of the binoculars. There were dozens of the animals, milling around the girl. She was now no more than a pale blob among all those eyes lit up like flames to watch her hungrily. Santelices was about to lean forward and shout a warning to her, but suddenly the window glass of "Leiva Brothers" lit up across from him and the doors opened with a whoop, as a cackle of vulgar laughter broke the air, resounding from place to place and shattering the heavy silence of his building. Santelices got his hat in the darkness and left.

That evening, he didn't eat at the house. The next day, however, he went straight home from work, found Bertha and told her that he had found a new place to live and since he'd be moving in a month, she could start advertising the room to be rented.

"But Santelices, why?" she babbled. "What . . . what have we done?"

"Nothing."

"But . . . then I don't understand . . ."

"Well, it's just that a woman from the office has a room to let and—she's a widow, you see—the room is in her apartment and she's offering it to me. She has no children and the apartment is quite nice, luxurious and modern. I would be her only boarder. Imagine the convenience, and this lady is so congenial. She plays guitar, you know . . ."

Livid, Bertha was breathing heavily as if something were building up in her, filling her up, until she sputtered, "You people always . . . go where the grass is greener . . . ungrateful . . . go ahead, leave if you want to! What's it to me? After the nice way we've treated you here in this house . . . what do I care? You're just like all men, you're filthy, interested in only one thing, filthy, nasty . . ." and she began to go to pieces, shaken with uncontrollable sobs.

A wall which had been building up for a long time in Santelices kept him from being affected. He did not hate her, nor wish her any harm, nor did he really have any plans to move out. But he realized that all he'd wanted for the longest time was to see this with his own eyes: Bertha, breaking down, crying desperately, and to know that he had caused it. Before the waves of his own natural compassion should flood him and dissolve the wall, he left. Outside, nothing mattered to him, absolutely nothing. Consoled, he went up to his own room.

He lay down on the bed without undressing. He could hear a tenant snoring in the next room. In another room, a child woke up and told his mother he wanted to go peepee. Some late returning tenants were tiptoeing up to their rooms, waking the old, creaky floorboards from their sleep.

Santelices contemplated the blank walls where for one night not so long ago, his obedient beasts had camped, all of them destroyed now by Bertha. It didn't matter anymore. For now the jungle was growing within him, with its heat and its roars and its strange outpouring of death and life. But something, yes, *something* mattered to him. In the depth of his imagination, as in the depth of a dark patio, a pale white blob was growing, the form of a girl surrounded by the terror of marauders on the prowl. She thought they were only cats, yes, just like the one on the front of the box of chocolates tied with blue ribbon, but no, he needed to shout her a warning; it was the only way to save her from being devoured. He couldn't sleep from thinking about the girl calling out to him in the night, imploring him, only him to help her. He tossed and turned on his bed, still with his clothes on, and he couldn't force out of his mind the thought of those dangerous beasts. He got up, swallowed a few times, for his throat was very dry. He started out, descending the stairs at a run, not caring about the noise he made and that his clattering footsteps were waking every tenant in the house. He had to hurry.

As he passed Bertha's door, she snapped on the light and shouted, "Santelices?"

He stopped and stood there without answering.

"Santelices! Where are you going this time of night, for the love of God!"

After a few seconds of silence, he answered in a strange voice, "I have to go out."

Closing the door behind him, he heard an animal-like cry that rasped the night, "Father!"

Outside, the cold air cut through his body, separating him from everything with a sort of fatal finality. In spite of the dry, windless cold, he took off his hat and let the air caress his neck, his throat, his brow, his bald head. It removed him, took his mind off the worry of the young girl who was about to be devoured.

He raced up the stairs to his office, opening one door after another without even being aware of what he was doing. At last he was there. In the darkness, he threw open the enormous, double window, letting it open up all the vast darkness of the colorless sky, where glowed a red-hot moon with fuzzy borders that looked like an abscessed inflamation that was about to burst and drip all over the tops of the gigantic trees beneath him. He choked back a cry of terror. The patio was thick with jungle cats, and their many eyes—yellow, granite, green, gold—were all staring at him. He covered his ears with his hands to shut out the roars that were bursting his eardrums. Where was the girl? Where was her lithe form among the foliage, the putrid air? Huge tigers with glowing eyes jumped from atop the stucco wall and down to the patio. Ocelots, hungry pumas, clawed the shreds of darkness among the violet leaves. The leopards were mauling the lynxes, the panthers were climbing the trees that almost, almost reached up to where Santelices was, as he scanned the patio with the binoculars in search of the girl. He still couldn't find her. Everything crackled and roared, trembling with insects crazy with the danger in the turbid, poisonous jungle air. From a nearby branch, a jaguar tried to bite Santelices on the hand, but its power could not extend beyond the limits of the binoculars. A furious panther with jeweled eyes like burning coals roared in front of his face.

Santelices was not afraid. He felt a need; it was imperative that he find his bravery in glorious triumph, in the most rich and ambitious way, unique in being so hard to define. There was a clearing below in the distance, in the farthest corner of the patio. Santelices caught his breath. It was she, yes, she who called to him to rescue her from that dreadful multitude of animals whose names she didn't even know, that were creeping, climbing from the trembling branches, as the birds ruffled their magnificent feathers among the monstrous ferns. His hands sweating, he slapped at the sticky bugs, moist from the hot, humid air. The whole night was aflame with eyes, up there in the sky across the giant branches that engulfed him, down to the tempest of swarming felines below that were now mangling each other furiously.

The heavy night air, barely illuminated by the translucent moon—or was it the sun in disguise?—was thick with howls trapped in its denseness. There was the girl waiting for him. Perhaps she was moaning; he couldn't hear her voice over the roaring and the growling, but he knew he had to save her. Santelices stepped out onto the ledge. Yes, there she was, directly below him. With a scream to drive off the great cat on the branch near her, he gave a furious leap down, down to where she was waiting.

Luis Domínguez

was born in 1933 in Santiago and has been a lawyer, a journalism professor, and, in various universities in the United States, a professor of Hispanic literature. Among his works are a novel, *Los Peces de color,* and two books of short stories, *El Extravagante* and *Citroneta blues.*

DUO

HE could always be found at Il Bosco, at the same table, with the same old crowd. Maybe a few more, a few less, a table or two over to the right or the left, but it was all the same: round table, dark red table-cloth, wine, conversation chewed around with the bread, the cheese, the cold cuts, above the glasses and the voices, and the nights didn't add up, but just ran into each other until they were all one.

Gaspar would go to those silly little celebrations with the white wine and oysters, but now nobody paid much attention to him. The last one for him had been for the success of his book, *Bad Conscience;* he remembered the voices resounding above the empty shells, all the voices of his poems. And when the bottles were all empty, Aldo coming around muttering almost in Gaspar's ear: "I gotta clean up this mess; I don't know how and I don't know what for." And that night, he had undressed in the dark, so as not to wake up Judith, even though later, after he was in bed, he had pressed up close to her until his body was against hers and she'd sighed; then, when his arm was around her and he had buried his breath in her hair, she'd turned over and murmured, "You smell like the sea."

Tonight, Gaspar didn't go in to Il Bosco. Instead, he stood for a few minutes on The Avenue, facing it, but he'd been seen there so many times that now nobody could say for sure that he'd been there on such and such a night or if he even had to keep going to be one of the crowd, and now he found himself looking at the group of women hanging around outside. He caught the eyes of one of them, eyes that looked like Judith's—insistent and smiling—and he didn't notice right then that it was she who had drawn his attention, not the other way around; you see, since his high school days he'd had a habit of looking around him to see if a nod or a wink were intended for someone else, before assuring himself that it really was for him.

They ended up walking in the same direction; she was walking farther away, with slow steps—he'd thought it was Judith and that he would surprise her. Now he was walking beside her and he realized she was taller than Judith, in fact, that the only thing that resembled her was that way she had of cutting her eyes at him—and maybe the shape of her legs. "You dance, don't you?"

"No, this is my job."

"But I'll bet you've danced before. You must have been a dancer someplace." He kept looking at her legs, and began playing with the change in his pocket. It was a game he liked—to play heads or tails—by the touch you guess whether it's heads or tails, two of a kind or two out of three. Solemnly they walked towards London Street. The jingling of the change in his full pocket sounded clearly in the still night. She bit her lower lip.

"What's your name?" he asked her.

"Flor . . and yours?"

"Gaspar Vega."

"You look like a poet."

He wanted to laugh. She would confess to him now that she didn't know anything about poetry, and that would be even better. Without even trying, he'd acquired the face of a poet. He wanted to tell her about the interviews, the poems from *Bad Conscience,* the green poster of himself where his eyes looked so wild and his lips were pressed together so that he looked as if he'd suddenly been confronted with some unspeakable horror. The seven-year, avant-garde, "Gaspar Vega or the passionate disease," some poems set to guitar, and the first bed with Judith, going on nineteen years, and the time on the mattress when they'd jerked apart to look for a bug between the blankets.

In the hotel, Flor went ahead of him down the hall. He was jingling the money in his pocket and thinking about Judith's legs, like a dancer's and smoother, he was sure. He pressed the coins against his wallet to make them stop jingling. As if in that pocket, he were clutching all his future meals in Il Bosco. (In school they'd called him "Jingle-pockets." Once in a TV interview, he'd said that since a child he'd liked to feel the change in his pockets; he thought it was because his family had been poor.)

He paid the desk clerk for the room and felt his change again. When it started jingling, Flor turned suddenly and said,

"You have to pay me first."

"No kidding?"

"It's the norm."

"Always?"

"Mmmm. Aren't you one of the bunch from Bosco?"

"I always go to the Bosco."

He sat down on the edge of the bed and began to tell her about the group, about Garmendia who was translating Ferlinghetti for an Argentinian press; about Enrico (some Antonian-Santiaguan type) who only needed a producer to make his screenplay a hit; about Matt Hernandez, a bad painter, who does posters to make a living; about Aldo Fuentes, author of *Cópula*, a pornographic novel, whose first printing had been held up by some incredibly bad luck (it'd go to press as soon as Aldo revised the last few chapters and changed some of the scenes); and then there was Mardones . . . just an ex-philosophy professor who was unfairly expelled from the University, and he's always good for a chat . . . but Judith had never had any respect for any of his friends . . .

Drops of sweat broke out on his brow and he felt a tingling all over his body. Now, naked to the waist, he was sitting on the bed, silently, not wanting to talk anymore. He noticed his face in the mirror and stared at it.

"... in every dream another dream and a
mirror in another mirror and in the mirror
the dream and another . . ."

"What'd you say?" she asked.

Gaspar looked over his shoulder, and it gave him a start, once more; she looked so much like Judith. But Flor had bigger, fuller breasts than Judith's, and longer legs. Half undressed, she came towards him. He was distracted. In the mirror, he saw himself more depressed than ever, and excessively white below the line of his shirt collar. Flor, standing in front of him, was playing with her locks of hair, flipping them into his face. He began to feel himself getting hard. A cold chill raised goose bumps on his arms.

"A woman left you, didn't she, Gaspar?" she asked softly, pulling his head toward her thighs. He took her in his arms then, rubbing his face against her thighs and kissing the bare flesh above the tops of her black stockings. Panting softly, he tried to take off her slip, but she wouldn't let him.

"So that's all it is?" she whispered, smiling. "How long has it been?"

He lifted his head and now she seemed like a strange woman again, not at all like Judith. This girl was young, and big, not more than twenty years old, with firm, hard lips and a tough look. He tried to start a conversation by asking how she knew so much about him, but she interrupted.

"Okay, okay, are you ready? Don't think I'm going to spend the whole night with you."

He started teasing her again to take off the rest of her clothes. He was standing beside the bed now. She dropped down on it and stretched out, beautiful with her red lips and long black hair, black slip and stockings as black as her hair and eyes. Pleading with her, Gaspar sat down beside her and starting tugging at her slip.

She was irritated. "Don't pull on me, hey, okay, I know how to undress by myself!" She jumped off the edge of the bed and headed for the bathroom.

Gaspar, quiet and depressed, watched her disappear. Maybe she was cold-natured. Judith, for instance, liked to take a bath at nighttime. Then she would come running to bed half-wet, dampening the sheets and making their bodies stick together. He would end up having to dry her. "All right, that's enough," she'd say, and "Be careful, you're squashing me!"

Gaspar took off his socks and shoes. He took his wallet and change from his pocket and left them on the lampstand. (He never played for money with anyone; his family had been so poor as he was growing up that he had always been plagued with the fear of losing it. The fear would go away, though, when he would play with his change, as if feeling the money in his hands would reassure him.) His pants fell to the floor and he picked them up, folding them absentmindedly as if his thoughts were somewhere else.

Before he could get another glimpse of her, Flor was in the bed. "Hurry up. It must be a long time since you've had a nude woman."

The bed was icy; so were her breasts and thighs. The first warmth came from her soft arms on his neck. She kissed his neck, imprisoning him between her thighs. He tried to kiss her on the belly and down her body, but she was in control and she stopped him, cradling his head between her breasts, "Pretend that I am that woman," she murmured. Gaspar looked down at her face, then slid his hand down her whole body, surprising that lower lip of hers that was now trembling in her baby face. "Gaspar, I know that when someone leaves someone, the one that's left keeps wanting the one that left," she whispered, agitated now, her words shortened by her quick breathing. His excitement was coming slowly. Now, he searched for hers. With both hands, he was caressing her everywhere until suddenly he felt her stiffen as if she herself were imprisoned within her own body. "Okay, come on," she sighed. He opened her cold legs that were trembling and rode her with slow, soft movements that began to be faster; she was helping him on, but letting him take over. With great effort, he stifled the words that came to his lips, burying his face in the pillow. She kissed him on the cheek, and they both relaxed, their sweat mingling together until they were bathed in the same warm damp.

He felt as if he were part of her. Ever so softly, he bit that lower lip of hers that was trembling so petulantly. She held him locked in her arms. All this time, he'd managed to swallow all his words to keep from saying the dreaded one. She murmured, "There was no one . . ."

Gaspar was still on top of her, his head buried in her hair. Their limp caresses became more and more languid until they were dozing. Finally, she said softly, "I wanted to make you speak a name . . ."

"I don't know what you're talking about," he answered. She fell into sleep then, as if she'd lost all her strength.

When Gaspar began to wake up, she was still nude, curled up like a baby, her back to him. In wonder, Gaspar raised up on his elbow and looked at her. Impulsively, he brought his lips close to her ear and whispered, "And you—why didn't *you* speak a name?"

"Nobody . . . never," she murmured.

The next time Gaspar woke up, he felt as if he'd slept too long. Flor was still sleeping too, and he could hear her light, faint, audible breathing. Her legs apart, one foot dangled off the bed. He kissed her at the base of the neck and behind the ears. Then he began moving his mouth down her body. She rolled over and tried to push him off, protesting, "No, no, I'm a—" but he covered her mouth with his, covered the curves of her open body; his head between her legs he began to hear her soft distant sighs and he raised his head to feel her moving desperately, agitatedly, her closed eyes at the verge of tears, as if searching for something, until finally he ended with his head buried in her rich black hair, smelling her whole body in it. Her throbbing sex was like an imprisoned mad thing freeing itself, recuperating from its wounds in a long, painful return to sanity.

"Flor," he murmured.

She pulled away from him and looked into his eyes. "You, what's—your name?"

"Gaspar, I told you."

"I've forgot everything and stayed here with you."

"What *is* everything?"

"I don't know, I just . . . forgot."

He pulled her to him, kissing her on the lips with short, tiny kisses. Little by little they fell asleep together. Night passed into morning and their intertwined arms and legs slipped slowly apart.

Near dawn, their heavy sleep had pulled them down deeper until they looked like two dead bodies. The only difference was that from time to time a murmur of a word or a syllable would escape the half-open lips; then sleep would fall over them again.

Gaspar woke up freezing. Her fragrance was clinging to the sheets and the pillow, but opening his eyes to the bright light of day he could see that she was gone. He looked for her with sincere anguish. He went to the bathroom, opened the window and looked out into the street. He didn't even think what a spectacle he must be, standing there nude at the window. He got dressed. Stuffing his tie into his jacket, he ran down the stairs and out. He checked his steps finally and walked, stopping in front of the church of San Francisco. The fresh air of seven in the morning in the Alameda was sharp in his nostrils and throat. He breathed deep. On the steps he saw two or three holy women, some newspaper sellers, and a couple of beggars. He walked on and stopped in front of Il Bosco. Bringing his hands to his face he sniffed them. A coalminer waiting for a bus regarded him with curiosity.

At the table inside the Bosco, he smiled. "Yes, yes, Aldo, I know I'll see her again. She's different. No, Mateo, it's not the same old story—go ahead, laugh if you want to—I'll find her again and then we'll see."

"Can I help you, sir?" spoke the waitress at his elbow. He piddled with his order, coffee and a roll. He dawdled over eating it; he kept looking at his watch. Aldo was starting to mutter about the oysters and the tables, "I gotta clean up this mess; I don't know how and I don't know what for."

Putting his hand in his pocket, Gaspar felt himself grow cold. The bitch! That bitch! he thought. His change and his wallet were gone. Sweat broke out all over his body and he gritted his teeth. Then, the feeling went away. He relaxed. His wallet and change were in the other pocket. He pressed the coins against the leather and smiled at his own foolishness. That morning, he must have moved them to the other pocket. Everything was all right. Everything was in order. Well, not quite in order. His money was in the wrong pocket. He remembered the TV interviewer saying something about the selfishness of money. But Gaspar had argued this and had said that money was a way of making contact with others. "A man without money is the most alone," he'd said. "For me, it represents the possibility of relationships; it's an antidote to loneliness."

That morning, at Il Bosco, he sat frowning, his elbows on the table, and wrote "Duo," a short poem, published in *Arbol de Letras* much later:

> Each age doubled is time gained,
> and in your eyes, nostalgia remains
> if each day there's no other face
> but yours, the one forgotten and eaten away,
> age undoubling, nothing remains

As he left Il Bosco, whistling, he walked down the Alameda toward his apartment on Lastarria. He was carrying a packet of oysters and a bottle of white wine. His one-day growth of beard made his face look a bit gray; the wind had disheveled his black hair. From one of his pockets dangled about seven or eight inches of a blue tie and his coins jingled in the other. It was early and nobody in the *barrio* recognized him.

He climbed the steps two by two and, right in front of the door, he ran into a woman in a black dress. He couldn't see her well in the darkness. "You, is it . . . you?"

"Yes, Gaspar, it's me."

"Oh, it's you. What'd you come here for?"

"Well I dreamed something bad had happened to you and I . . ."

"Something bad?"

"Yes, I had a nightmare, and . . ."

"Nothing bad has happened to me. In fact, . . ."

"Are you mad that I came here?"

"No . . . no, come in."

Gaspar pressed the bottle and the oysters against his chest, freeing his right hand to get the key out of his pocket. In doing so, he jerked the coins along with it, and as he opened the door, they fell all over the floor. But he continued as if he'd not even heard them fall. "Come in, come in," he insisted, trying to see her eyes in the darkness. Judith was kneeling, picking up the coins.

José Luís Rosasco

was born in Santiago in 1935. He still resides there as director of the Sociedad de Escritores de Chile. He is also a member of the Committee of Literature at the Instituto Chileno Nortamericano de Cultura.

Rosasco has published four books of short stories. *Hoy día es mañana*, which contains the story translated here, was published in 1980. His first novel, *Dónde estás Constanza*, was also published in 1980 and obtained the Andrés Bello Novel Award. Other awards, for various works of short fiction include the Gabriela Mistral in 1969, the Pedro de Oña in 1970 and the Premio Municipal de Santiago in 1972. His stories have been translated into English, French, and Portuguese.

DAMELZA

I MET Damelza at a restaurant in Greenwich Village. In the sixties, at the turn of the decade, the Village was still a place where you could live on a few dollars a day, if you could find, for example, a little apartment for less than two hundred fifty a month. Of course, the closer you got to the Puerto Rican section, the more bearable the rent became. I figured that if I could settle for the cheapest place I could find, I'd be able to afford, among other luxuries, a once-a-week splurge in a good Italian restaurant, or Greek, or Chinese. The Sheila-Fu, a block from Washington Square, was Chinese all the way, and it was there that I met Damelza.

It was the first time that I had ever been there. I'd only been in the United States for two months, and the description of the Chinese dishes, in English, were presenting painful difficulties. I assumed that the Chinese waiter had arrived in the United States years before I had, but his idiomatic ineptitude couldn't have been more abominable. I was at the point of arbitrarily ordering anything on the menu, when a young woman who occupied a nearby table caught my attention with a smile and a slight questioning look that indicated she might help me out of this jam. I nodded enthusiastically, and ventured to gesture her over to my table, since it was evident to both of us that we were alone. She accepted immediately and at once began to interpret the menu while I devoted my attention to studying her perhaps too deeply.

It was just that she was so beautiful. It wasn't easy to decide just how old she was; she could have been, say, over thirty, but then again, maybe younger than that. She was tall and blonde, one of those types who manage to stay young-looking by the grace of a fresh, healthy complexion, a pert little turned-up nose, and that way she had of swishing her ponytail. In her eyes, though, there lurked something from another dimension. Not that they lacked vitality, far from it, nor was there any blemish of yellow or red in the whites of them, no, nothing like that. It's just that they were continually moist, and strangely enough, that watery film blended so well with their green color that the effect was that they seemed always to show something of a mature sadness.

Soon we found ourselves engaged in lively conversation. It's possible that our gaiety was partly brought on by the bottle of California Chianti she had ordered (to neutralize the oil and the soy sauce, she said), at least it was for her. As for me, my tongue had wanted loosening for two months; the loneliness within me had accumulated its forces to the breaking point; I had found no one to talk to; in fact, I had even lost touch with my two classmates from Latin America, since I had dropped the two literature courses they were in.

I told Damelza that she had a lovely name. Since we were alone I called her by name; though at her house they would call her Mrs. Stanley, all except for her husband, of course. Christopher Stanley was, at that time, a prominent professor of literature, well-known not only at N.Y.U., but elsewhere as well. He had written a book about the beatnik generation, and it had soon become a favorite topic of conversation, a well-liked text, first by the students, and later, when a commercial press decided to pick up on it, it was received by the public with astonishing popularity. I've browsed through it a few times over the years, and I have to admit it reads well; that's all I can say for it.

Well, it so happened that on that first occasion Damelza invited me to her house. "I'd like it very much if you could come to visit us," she said. "We receive guests every Friday evening. My husband is biased toward foreigns; he would enjoy meeting you, and you'll get to meet some people that have things in common with you. But don't think we're all so formal and serious; we just talk and listen to music, dance sometimes. We have a good time."

I had just told her about some of my work, and I believe that her interest was really sincere, and that she really did want to see some of my stories. Actually, she would have no reason to pretend; she'd only met me a couple of hours ago.

We said goodnight at the subway entrance in Washington Square. She kissed me on the cheek. "Until next Friday, then," she said. As she went down the steps, she called after me, "I'll be expecting you!" A sharp December wind with a warning of snow blew away my last reflections of Damelza and her pony-tail, which had just disappeared among the crowd.

The Stanleys lived on Staten Island. It might seem strange, but there were a lot of things about the island which reminded me of the place I had come from. My childhood and adolescence had taken place in a Santiago *barrio,* unselfish and free from restraint. It was a place of gardens, squares and courtyards, trees with wide spaces between them, and untouched virgin land. Above it all there floated the rich, intimate harmonious spirit of the suburbs, characteristic of any village boundary, where the presence of nature still exists unhampered by traffic, by pavements, by the noisy multitudes and their games, by the limits of the sights of the short-sighted.

I would speak to Damelza often of my nostalgia. Countless times, after she started coming to see me, I would talk about it, and I know I must have abused her tolerance at great length. There were entire afternoons that I spent describing to her the surroundings of my district. The cattle barn three blocks from our house, those men who would pass through the street selling turkeys and waving little whips, the organ grinders whose music was rarely spoiled by a sour note, the dogs that kept crossing the streets with never any fear of being run over, the laundress who would bring the clothes in a basket on her head—and they always smelled like smoke—the '29 taxi that would spend entire afternoons parked beside its owner's house on the corner of the plaza, the strange attraction of the drainage ditches . . .

It's true that by the time I had come to the United States most of those things were already gone from the *barrio,* but they still existed vividly in my memory, the memory of my childhood, and it was those memories that New York had unloosed in me with such powerful importance. I know that many of those long afternoons must have been terribly tedious for Damelza, but I also know that her tolerance was part of her nature.

The Stanleys' house, like so many others on Staten Island, was a two-story wood structure. The ground floor opened into a receiving room where you could see the stairway that led up to the second floor. The receiving room connected on one side with the professor's study, and on the other with the spacious living room and equally large dining room that looked out onto the back yard. The rooms were comfortably large, enough so as to allow the Friday afternoon guests to move about easily from one place to another. Usually, Professor Stanley could be found in the library with a couple of students, a writer, a critic, or some academician of renown.

On my first visit, Damelza had told me that, since so many people were always getting off the ferry, I should call her from the telephone booth where the cars pick up passengers. This I did.

"Fantastic! You're here!" she exclaimed. "I'll send for you at . . . oh, forget it! Listen, why don't you wait out there by the traffic circle at the entrance; somebody will come by for you in my car, it's an antique Pontiac, yellow, 1950. There's no other one like it on the island. See you."

Fifteen minutes later, I saw the Pontiac pull up. I opened the door and sat down by the driver, an Italian-looking guy, apparently fairly tall, with wavy hair abundantly sprinkled with silver at the temples (the most attractive feature about his television announcer's face).

I noticed that he had had a little to drink. "Since you're the latest acquisition of Mrs. Stanley," he said in a conversational tone, "you can call me Dan. Dan Corso, writer, nobody knows me of course, but I've written the hottest novel of our time. Nobody wants to publish it, but don't worry, I'm getting rich writing screenplays for TV. A hell of a job! But they, the producers I mean, are loaded."

"Well, soon you'll be able to finance the publication of your own novel," I said.

"Never! Listen, son, the day will dawn when Mailer, Bellow, and Salinger, and who knows what other clowns out there will come begging for my autograph." He kept on talking disjointedly on different subjects until we reached the Stanleys' house. "Before we go in, there's just one thing. Don't forget to talk to the old man, you hear? Lend him an ear; everybody does, understand? It won't take much of your time and it'll make him happy; besides, he always brings in some tedious bastard to lend a little weight to the conversations. Okay?"

I left Dan Corso's car, greatly disconcerted; his manner of referring to the owner of the house seemed to me openly vulgar and impertinent. A student met us at the door and Corso went lumbering like a horse into the receiving room and on through to the living room. I could hear him saying, "Here's the new Latino, Chileno, Brasileño, Paragueño, or how should I know . . ." And laughter resounded around him.

Damelza came up to me just then, and Professor Stanley appeared from the library. "How are you, Alex?" he asked, and clasped my hand in a warm handshake. "Damelza has told me about you. I'm sure we'll have plenty of opportunities to talk later. I'm happy to hear you're studying literature at N.Y.U. What I mean is, maybe in a couple of years you'll be a student of mine." With a smile, he added, "if you choose me, that is. You can choose your own courses, you know, your own professors, I should say."

"Of course I would choose you, sir," I said.

"Well, come on, Alex, that remains to be seen. One thing at a time, but before you go on into Damelza's zoo, tell me, do you miss your country—your people—a lot?"

"Yes, sir, as a matter of fact, I do," I told him.

"Magnificent!" he said, motioning me into the living room. "Magnificent, Alex, because do you know what? Nostalgia is one of the most fertile territories for a writer to work in. See now, Damelza has told me that you write—come on inside, young man."

The abrupt entrance of Dan Corso, the presence of Damelza, the words of Professor Stanley, and later, the introductions and conversations in the living room had not given me much time to ponder what had been the effect of my initial meeting with the professor. Later, hours later, alone in my room in the Village, I would devote myself to reliving the scenes of the evening.

It was the image of Damelza that kept intruding into my thoughts: of her moving from one place to another, conversing and attending to the guests, which were her guests, actually. This image of her captured all the attention of my musings. Her figure, her lithe body which was so much more agile than I had imagined that day at the Sheila-Fu. Her flesh was youthful, hard, firm. Her age seemed more indeterminable than ever. Seeing her among so many young people, I found her energy no contrast; on the contrary, it equalled and surpassed that of the young men.

Damelza had given me more attention than the rest, presumably because it was my first time there, but that might not have been the reason. That preference could have been, perhaps, my singularity of character, and this thought flattered me. I wanted to feel that that was it, and so I did. It had not escaped my attention that all of us present had been men, a fact which was regrettable.

In the whole two months that I had been here so far, I had not been able to find, nor did I hope to anymore, a female friend who could become like a companion. Where was all that North American female accessibility and liberality, that openmindedness toward foreign people that was so freely talked about back home? That evening, at the party, I had brought up this whole topic with a short Mexican fellow with a big head. He had been in New York for over a year, and seemed to be fairly loose-mouthed, so I asked him if girls ever came to the Stanleys' house parties. "Never, hombre," he said. "Mrs. Stanley is the Queen Bee, understand?" It was the same kind of "understand" that Dan Corso had given me, one of those that says everything without saying anything openly.

"Well, what a pity!" I said. "It would be a lot more fun if other women came too, wouldn't you think?"

He laughed uproariously. "What a scream!" he exclaimed. "You're pretty new here, and among other things, I'll bet you've never made it with a *gringa,* have you?" Somewhat embarrassed, I admitted that I hadn't. "Well, don't feel like the only duck in the pond on that score," he said. "Anyhow, you haven't missed anything—it's not what it's cracked up to be. They're something else! Hang me if they're not! You want to hear about it?"

I was interested.

"Okay, you invite your prime subject for the first date, and, listen to this, your highlight of the evening, if you can call it that, might be a good night kiss. But that doesn't mean a thing, for them I mean, and look; you can even spend a weekend, go everywhere with 'em, and nothing will happen, nothing, that is, in a manner that—you want me to give you some advice?"

"Go on."

"When you go out with a *gringa,* leave your heart on the doorstep. Now that doesn't mean that we're among celestial beings, no sir, things do happen, and when they do, they happen all the way, but that's all part of the sport, understand?"

I understood perfectly, and it seemed to me that given my situation, I would have no objections to the sport.

"Where are you living?" he asked me, as if to change the subject.

"I've got a little kitchenette near the university, towards third Avenue."

"Near the Village!" he shouted, his voice in his throat. "But man, you're an idiot, if you can't make something out of that! That's THE place. Hey, Mrs. Stanley!" he called. "Did you know your Chilean friend lives in the Village?"

Damelza approached us. "Yes, I knew that."

"And did you know he lives there like a monk?"

"I wouldn't necessarily know that."

"Friend," said Bighead, "I'm going to pay you a visit soon."

"What for?" asked Damelza.

"Well, to introduce him to the place. This poor guy is living in the oven, and complaining of the cold!"

"I'm not complaining," I said, irritated.

"In any case," Damelza went on, "I don't think you'd be the best one to initiate Alex into that maze."

"Who would be better, then?" asked Bighead.

"I would," she affirmed, and, winking at me, turned and headed for the dining room.

"You're a smart one, Chileno," Bighead said, grinning lewdly, "but don't get any illusions."

I wanted to know what he meant by that.

"Oh, it's just a general word of warning; you see the girls around here; they're not like ours. They don't treat you the way a man ought to be treated. For instance, when you go to a girl's place, what happens, in Chile or in Mexico, where the girls have that certain feminine quality, that 'always wanting to please,' so they offer you something to eat, something to drink, they bend over backwards to try to make you feel like the *macho* guy you are. And here? All you get is that casual 'help yourself.' I mean it's like 'get along by yourself,' 'serve yourself,' 'entertain yourself,' 'fix-up yourself a drink,' etc. And after that, friend, on top of all that, do you think a girl from this country is gonna want to wash your handkerchiefs and your underwear? Have a seat; it'll be a long wait."

I remembered my trip on the *Chilean Nitrate*. We had gotten on the ship at San Antonio. Suddenly I was re-living all of it. At the port, the image of my mother waving a damp handkerchief, the figure of my brother, standing erect, and calm, Carmen with her eyes large and round like black grapes and our broken relationship.

I was standing with my foot on the rail—I remember that later the boat had started to vibrate from beneath like a huge submerged lung, and the port had gotten farther away since it seemed that it was the port and not the boat that was moving. And how later, in the next few days . . . what was it Bighead had been talking about? Oh yes, about washing the underwear. And later, in the next few days, I, the ultra-macho Chilean that I was, throwing my old underwear into the sea . . .

"You know," I told Bighead, "I got to New York without a single pair of underwear."

"What are you talking about?"

"I said I got here without any underwear. I'm talking about *machismo*."

"What's the matter with you, man?"

Now it was he who didn't understand.

About the middle of the next week Damelza came to my place for the first time. It was very cold; from the window I was watching the falling snow as it speckled the clearness of the day. My vision was blurred by the flakes that were coming down with such constance, filling me with dizzy meditation, something like the feeling one has when staring into flames or the sea. I lived on the first floor, so from time to time, the trance would be broken by the sound of someone's footsteps in the otherwise empty corridor.

Damelza's face, framed by a bright red hood, appeared through the windowpane, and her gloved hand knocked lightly on the outside door. I opened it, and she came into the hall. Now she was in the apartment, taking off her cape, and she told me that she had come to Manhattan just to see me.

"Let's see how you live," she said, moving through the dining room and living room, casting a quick glance into the bedroom that adjoined (actually these two little rooms had originally been one, but now they were separated by a partition of shelves, with a two-doored screen that opened out in the middle.

"What dreadful furnishings!" she exclaimed. "And this lamp! Jesus! There's nothing—I mean *nothing* worse than art nouveau—it's surprising how many blobs of it have survived in New York. I'd like to make a bonfire of all of them! No, I'm just kidding! How rude of me, Alex, I'm sorry; without this furniture, these boarding houses would be nothing; they'd lose—well, I don't know what, but something— that certain touch, like . . . something taken out of its time. You'd expect Humphrey Bogart to walk in here any minute. Alex, forgive me." She came close to me and, putting her hands on my shoulders, she kissed me on the forehead. "Nothing's wrong, there's nothing wrong with any of it, all right?" Without waiting for an answer, she turned and went into the kitchen.

"How awful! But how awful! All this mess and grease and dust, Alex, my God! Hand me a dishcloth—oh, I bet you don't have a clean rag on the place—tell me where you keep your dishwashing liquid; what a baby, how do they raise you lazy Latin bums; come on, where's the steel wool?"

"The what?"

"The steel wool! You know, to clean these pots with."

"Oh, heck. There isn't any," I said.

"Well, we'll do the best we can and you—go buy some steel wool, and . . . hey, what have you got to eat? I'm starving—I left Staten Island this morning with nothing in my stomach but a cup of coffee and the snow just makes me ravenous."

"I've got some cans of asparagus, some corn, some beans, some clam chowder . . ."

"No, I want something hot. Here." She handed me a ten-dollar bill. "Go buy some pizza, or better yet, some ravioli with sauce and a bottle of Chianti. You remember the brand that we had in the restaurant, Paul something or one like that. Okay, go ahead, go!"

I put on my raincoat and hat and went out. I looked back at Damelza from outside; I tapped on the window; she stuck out her tongue at me and waved me on with her hand.

While we ate, some of Damelza's vitality began to fall away. The more I got to know her, the more aware I became of her sudden changes of temperament from gaiety to depression, from a bubbling way of talking that was almost infantile to one of grave serenity. That was when she became most inquisitive; her curiosity about my former life was boundless. What were my parents like, my brother; who had been my best friends, my favorite teachers; where had we spent our summers; what had been my favorite TV programs before coming here; what had my high school been like; where in the United States did my Italian relatives live, and was I ever going to visit them; what was my house back home like; what trees did it have; and finally, the neighborhood—at the end of a month's time, I believe that Damelza knew about as much about me as a confidential friend would, because she also asked me very intimate questions. She shared the common opinion that Italian blood generated men who were extremely passionate, amorous, and violent. Even though my character denied this stereotype, Damelza insisted that these qualities slept deep within me. "I've had Italians," she affirmed. "I know how they are; I'm right about that."

She spoke of having men and of having had men in a way that disgusted me. I couldn't ignore the stamp of the professional trademark on those escapades, and the frivolousness of it all could not but repel me. I could not understand how she failed to recognize the degrading elements of her lifestyle that were so damaging to her character. Still, little by little, I found myself taking pleasure in her childish prattle, and I even began to encourage her in this diversion. In fact, in that episode of our lives prior to and even during our love affair, I understood intuitively that these conversations would inevitably open up to me the pathway to her eroticism.

I took advantage of one of those opportunities later to ask her about her relationship with Professor Stanley. By then it was midsummer. The heat and the humidity was another reason for us to be nude most of the time we spent at my place. We had made love that afternoon more passionately, more brutally than usual. It wasn't always like that. Damelza could be very tender—and when she was, we would lie there for long periods of silence; on the other hand, after wearing ourselves out in the ecstasy of our sensuality, we would try to find things to talk about.

"You never talk to me about Mr. Stanley," I said.

"You never ask me about him," she answered.

"Well, that's understandable," I retorted.

"Yes, sure it is. Okay, what do you want to know?"

"Everything."

"I was his student. I was alone; he took care of me. And I loved him, too. That's everything."

It was only natural that I no longer went very often to Staten Island. I let two or three weeks go by, but I didn't want to disappear completely from the scene. I could not rid myself of the feeling that I represented the evil force there. Not simply because the presence of Professor Stanley and his affability toward me sharpened my feelings of guilt, but also because Damelza was another person at her house, and that meant a lot of things. For example, there was Dan Corso, with his big mouth always open and flapping, and his nasty remarks, nourished by the effects of the liquor, and he was always carrying on in a very familiar way toward Damelza, stepping over that line of tactful discreteness with no regard for the code that ruled in the household. I had to admit, he was an ingenious character, and eventually I realized that he really was getting rich on his screenplays; a European convertible at the door and some lightning trips to California were undeniable facts.

Damelza treated him in a special way. Of course, this was not discernible to everyone, but it was to me, because I had begun to develop with respect to her a singular perception; not one detail escaped me, every trifling shade and turn of her temperament that I knew how to interpret cut me like a knife.

If I had ever before felt the pangs of jealousy, they had only been presented to me in certain situations, more or less removed, you might say, in circumstances where rules and rights were in their places, so that whatever altered what ought to be produced logical reactions, obvious reactions, in consequence. But what I was experiencing now couldn't have been more distant from, or more opposed to, that, shall we say, normality. My youth and inexperience swelled to a confusion, and my inward self struggled to redeem all that—that something, that sense of the ideal, of custom.

Also, I was overcome with the fear that someone might realize or perceive how much in love I was with Damelza. I believed I was safe in assuming that, except for Bighead, nobody had even the slightest reason to suspect it.

Bighead had now become a friend and confidant. He lived in a very economical tenement in Brooklyn. I believe that the reason for its being economical was that it was so far away, for Bighead would often spend the night at my place when it got too late. More than once our conversations lasted well into the morning hours. He maintained a critical attitude toward my relationship with Damelza, not toward the affair itself, but with regard to the fact, which painfully I acknowledged, that I was as lovesick as a schoolboy. He did not want to recognize that that was exactly what I was, that Damelza constituted for me my first adult love, and therefore I could not avoid involving myself in a deeply personal way.

Bighead also made me realize that it was not such a serious thing for her as it was for me. This fact became more painful to me as time went on; it was a truth that I preferred not to face, and one which troubled me to analyze. When he insisted along these lines, I would change the subject by leading him into recounting some of his own romantic adventures. He would then launch into the story of his adolescence in Puebla. It aways left me with the impression that a good part of his stories was pure fantasy; to believe it all would be to conclude that Bighead had been a real lady-killer in his country. I believe that the beer (I kept the Chianti for Damelza's visits) was overstimulating our imaginations and our nostalgia, especially after midnight. Bighead was an extraordinary listener; in fact he was even better than Damelza at drawing me out. He had a special knack for savoring every detail, and never again did I meet anyone like him who could speculate so amply on what was told him, especially where girls were concerned.

My romantic repertoire was not particularly extensive, but Bighead invariably convinced me otherwise. I had brought some photographs with me and he would look at the girls in them and categorize them according to their temperaments, based on the facial characteristics and their figures. Of course, it was all sheer coincidence, that in all this pretense there flowed a tiny current of validity, but it didn't matter. The most valuable part of it was that he was so able to get caught up in it and find diversion for himself.

He also devoured the letters that I continued to receive from Carmen, my most recent lover in Chile. For my part I must confess that the correspondence didn't cause me even the tiniest throb of nostalgia. What I really wished was that that sweet, loving, unshakably faithful girl would understand, in the most painless way possible, that Damelza left no room in my heart for anyone else. Of course, there was precious little that I had done through my letters to alleviate her pain. I knew that the sooner I entered into an explanation of the nature of my passion for Damelza, the sooner Carmen could start cutting the ties and letting her wounds heal, but I stalled about it, and kept on writing, answering her letters with a morbid sense of pleasure each time I mentioned Damelza's name. It was just that Damelza had such a hold on me. Compared to this experience, all my former ones seemed empty, gray, incomplete. The most that my present rapture would allow me to salvage from any of them was a sort of weak, skewed illusion of a happy memory. But not always. Carmen and I had made love in the hills of La Reina, above Santiago, in the eucalyptus forest. Those amorous sessions, in which she never completely disrobed, were always preceded by a struggle, with our wrestling accompanied by verbal utterances, with various manifestations of Good and Evil, Bertrand Russell, Christ, Mama, the Middle Ages, the twentieth century, and finally ending in a monstrous tangle from which we emerged weakened by the somewhat relevant, somewhat precarious pleasure.

Damelza, on the other hand, came to my bedroom and took off her clothes with the same casual naturalness with which she would uncork a bottle of Chianti. I don't know at what point the Chianti brought upon her that erotic condition of *sina qua non,* but I don't doubt that it played a heavy role. In a certain sense, I myself became permanently affected by the Chianti—over the years I have often been caught standing before the fireplace staring at a bottle of red wine left on the hearth, and when asked what I was thinking about I had to reply that the flames from the burning wood had attracted my concentration, like the waves of the sea or the falling snow.

Near the end of the winter, I received a positive stimulus, in the form of a part-time job on the university journal, under the direction of the cultural editor. My work, which took up four hours a day, consisted of receiving and doing the preliminary selecting of short fiction from the Spanish-speaking students, who numbered about three hundred. The editor had chosen me because of a story of mine that he himself had selected to publish. In addition to my other responsibilities, I was in charge of selecting texts to be reviewed, written by Spanish and Latin-American authors. The position was a very high honor, it didn't even seem like a job, really; I would learn a great deal, and it gave me some prestige among my friends and cohorts, besides a few extra dollars a month.

Needless to say, the first one to benefit from my newly acquired wealth was Damelza. Although I couldn't take her to the places that Dan Corso was always talking about, still we became connoisseurs of the best tables in the Village, Italian restaurants, Greek, Chinese, draining my pockets, I will say, on a regular basis.

The Village was now experiencing a change. The first hippies were beginning to drift in from California. It was an invasion that threatened an alteration in the whole cast of the area, something that had seemed so unshakable a few months before.

A certain academician, one of the more pompous guests of Professor Stanley, remarked that the whole hippie movement was apocalyptic. Professor Stanley discussed the point with him. "There's a certain elemental purity in those young people," he said.

Damelza smiled. "If I were ten or fifteen years younger, I'd be a hippie," she said.

"You might be—for a while," the professor remarked.

"Don't be so sure," she replied.

The most contented among us about the eruption of the hippies was Bighead. He could be found every night now haunting the streets around Washington Square. There was no getting lost for him.

Between 10th and 12th streets now, ground level restaurants were opening up, installing themselves beneath the streets with tunnels leading down, out of which poured blasts of strident music and great rolls of smoke, impregnated with the sharp aroma of marihuana. All this and the girls, with glassy eyes and no bras, were for Bighead, part of the lost Utopia. "Man, this is crazy!" he told me. "Now I know it was worth it to come here! Every *gringa* yields a harvest."

In a very short time, Bighead had begun to look like a wraith. Both Damelza and the professor called him severely to attention over it. It was clear that he had abandoned his studies and he looked as if he could come down with pneumonia at any moment.

"The hippies," Dan Corso decreed, "can't survive the climate here in New York. In San Francisco maybe, or the Caribbean, or even South America . . . hey, you Latins can take all the hippies with you when you go, how about that?"

His idiotic idea found a disciple, of all things, in the form of Big-head. A hippie from Arizona had fallen in love with him. She was a beautiful girl, barely fifteen years old, and was carrying his baby. One afternoon they came by my place, obviously nervous. They had come to say good-bye. Bighead had never mentioned this possibility to me, and he felt as if he had been betraying me by keeping the secret so long. Even though I was going to miss him terribly, I could not help but feel that the decision was unquestionably the best thing for both of them. Bighead was wasting away in New York, and as for the girl, she would never hold up in the Village with its nightlife that had by some stroke of fortune brought them together. The sun, the air, the provincial rhythm of Puebla, should sober them both. Of course I could not say whether or not she would be able to leave her former life behind her and settle in Mexico, but if they could trust in each other enough to try to establish themselves there, with that initial force born of the rejection they were now experiencing in New York, then of course, the baby that she was carrying in her womb would serve as a powerful fountain of strength and serenity.

"I'm going to settle down," he said. "Isn't it funny how many turns there are to life? Me, a lady-killer, a Don Juan that came here looking for God knows what, going home a daddy? We're going to be married in the Cathedral of Puebla."

"Ave Maria."

The girl smiled.

"You'll come by and see us on your way home to Chile, won't you?"

"Sure, man."

"You want to hear a good idea," he asked me.

"Of course, Bighead. What is it?"

"Get yourself a little girl like this one."

I couldn't resist a jibe. "You had a pretty different opinion of American girls before, in case you haven't forgotten."

"Well, that was before," he affirmed, in the tone of someone speaking of the distant past. Then he added. "A woman can change a man, you know—she can return him to Paradise Lost."

That seemed a little too much for me, but I brought forth no objections. It was plain that love was distorting his whole concept of reality. For a few minutes, I was almost happy about it, and I felt like a sententious old auntie.

"So how's Damelza?" he asked.

"She's fine, she was here last night. We went to the Sheila-Fu, to reminisce about the first time we ever met. We like to do that every once in a while."

"Listen, man, can I tell you something?"

"Sure."

"Leave that woman. She's no good for you; there's no future in any of that."

"I'm an existentialist. I'm only interested in the here and now."

"Alex, let me give you some advice—"

"No! Shut your mouth or change the subject." I had loved the old Bighead who was now dying; it was he who had been my friend, my companion, my confidant. "We could go to a movie," I said, "down at Eighteenth and Casablanca." The girl agreed. Bighead said that was a good idea.

When summer came, I received an invitation from my Italian relatives who lived in Washington. We had written consistently, and they insisted that I come and spend a couple of weeks with them. To do this, I'd have to leave immediately, since they planned to spend the rest of their vacation in Florida. Because of Damelza, I'd been putting off the trip, and even now, I would have preferred not to leave, but it was she who urged me to accept the invitation.

"A change of atmosphere would do you good," she said. "Washington is a beautiful city; it has something of the enchantment of the South, and something of the antiquity of the North. Besides, you're tired; everyone is after a year of classes, and you especially with your job on the journal; you've had more than your share."

"I don't know," I said. "I was hoping maybe this summer you and I could spend more time together." I sincerely believed it. I had not enrolled in anything for summer school, and it was very likely that Professor Stanley would be doing some extra tutoring, which opened up all kinds of possibilities.

"I'm sorry, Alex, I really am sorry, but I'm going to be more busy than you can imagine this summer."

"Doing what? Are you going to replace someone?" She had told me once that she often filled in for secretaries on vacation; it paid double, and, except for registration, the work was pretty light.

"Yes, something like that, maybe."

"You're not even sure."

"Yes, I'm sure, love, I'm sure." She kissed me, a long kiss. "Besides, Alex," she said, "it might be a good idea for us not to see each other for a while."

"I don't know how you can say that; I would spend my whole life with you, and I'd always hate our having to be away from each other."

"Alex, you're starting to act silly and melodramatic, like a jealous Italian. It's only a question of a couple of weeks. Come on, be reasonable."

"It's plain to me that there's a big difference between the way I feel and the way you feel."

"Come on, man, what's this Mexican ballad you're singing? Here, strip me."

"Damelza."

"Yes, love."

"Tell me that you love me."

"Okay, I love you."

"Tell me that you love only me, that you belong to me."

"Man! Talk about a notion of private property! You're becoming an insufferable capitalist."

We fell locked in an embrace. It was a very amorous session of love-making, one that left me drained down to the depths of my body, but left my mind strangely clear, open, expectant, as if trying to ascertain something, affirm something, rest in something. Damelza's damp body lay absolutely inert, except for her breathing, which was the only perceptible sign of her still being alive. I lay looking at her, contemplating her, feeling my disgust at my abject slavery to that body, those curves, that bland warm flesh. Then I kissed her hands, her palms, her eyelids, her hair, wanting her to understand, to know that I had hidden myself in those places, as a way of showing her my adoration that lived so close, yet so far from the warmth of her blood, from the touch of her skin, from the contact of her whole body.

"Alex."

"Yes, beloved."

"You were formidable. Yes, you were formidable. I'm going to miss you. You were fierce."

I spent exactly two weeks in Washington. My relatives were a serene family. They lived in a spacious apartment on Pennsylvania Avenue, a few blocks from the White House; consequently, near all the parks, the monuments, the official buildings. My uncle Carlo, my father's brother, had married the daughter of some immigrants who were also Italian. There were two children, a fourteen-year-old son, whom I saw very little of, the only one in the family who actually violated the tradition of devoting all one's time to a new relative, and a sixteen-year-old daughter, Anna, in her last year of high school. Anna had plans to study foreign languages in some university in New York. Her mother was not favorable towards the idea of letting young people study in another city so far away from their parents' home. There was no doubt that she was going to lose this battle. Uncle Carlo maintained an apparently neutral position, but it was obvious that he wasn't thinking of opposing the idea.

"You've lived a while in New York," my aunt started in on me. "You can tell us how hard it is for girls who've been raised Italian. You could tell Anna that things are more or less, well . . . dangerous."

My aunt was putting me in an awkward and embarassing situation with that opening. Anna was looking at me with her enormous black eyes and I was sure that I saw something of a plea in them. My uncle tried to get me out of it: "Alex was also brought up in a Latin environment, love, and as you can see, he's still very sane."

"Let him speak for himself, Carlo. Come, Alex. You have to be honest about this with your aunt and uncle, with your cousin. You have to agree about the drugs, the rapes, and those hippies. Come on, Alex, tell the truth."

"Mama, for heaven's sake, you talk as if we lived in a little town. We have drug addicts and all that here, too."

"What we're trying to say, my dear," my uncle put in, "is that one should trust in the upbringing that we've given the children. There is where the true protection resides."

"Well then, Alex, say something. Tell us of your own experiences, since you're a man already, and I'm sure you've seen things—terrible things."

"I've seen everything, ma'am." I said.

"Girls that go astray?"

"And girls that live normally; actually, it depends on the person, on each one's—"

"Exactly!" my uncle jumped in. "And that's just what I was saying, Love, so that's enough of it—you're putting Alex on the spot. You must understand that a young man can't tell all of his—his amorous escapades, his—"

"Aha! And with whom do they have these escapades? With girls, girls who are alone, isn't that right? Tell me, Alex, do you have a girlfriend?"

"Aunt, of course I do. She's a friend, someone I met at school."

"Oh! Well, you're a good boy, anyone can see that, but—"

"This subject is closed," Uncle Carlo said firmly. "Go on, love, fix us something to eat now. Go ahead, go."

"All right I'm going. See, Alex, I have to give in to this *machismo* because that's the way I was raised. And that's all I've been trying to tell you. Everyone should follow the way he was raised, try to preserve that and not stray away from it."

Anna was beautiful. She had a glowing complexion of a smoothness and purity that had obviously never been touched by make-up. Her long black hair was thick and glossy, and her figure was slender and elegant, with curves that were modest but evident.

At first, during the first week, Anna was rather shy, but later she broke her reserve with me and I got to know her without reservations. She was very intelligent, much more so than her parents realized. She was determined to see the world; she wanted to be an interpreter. Besides English and Italian, the two languages she had been raised with, she had also taken up French and was learning Spanish on her own.

We went out together alone a couple of times. On one of those occasions, we left the outskirts of Washington, heading toward Cockeysville, the wild, uncivilized area of Maryland, where she had a girlfriend whom she owed a visit. It was a very sunny day. The three of us penetrated a pine forest, where the trees bristled between two hills, and there we found a clearing in which to rest and eat. As I opened the bottle of Chianti to go with our picnic, I thought of Damelza, and her image hung before me for a fraction of a second. At that moment, I realized how alien she was to me here on this green hillside with these two young girls. There was Anna, some years younger than I, just a few years, yes, but the crucial ones. She was so beautiful, so barely accessible, full of distant vitality, ready for any adventure, inviting as an outstretched hand, like the open horizon. Now she was cutting a melon on her lap, laughing aloud as she tried to do it with a pocket knife; one of the halves had slipped and the juice had stained her pants. She then offered me the biggest half. More laughter; we had forgotten the sugar for the coffee, but we were enjoying ourselves so it didn't matter.

Anna's friend was asleep so we took a walk in the woods, Anna and

I. The trees seemed to be losing their density and it became apparent that we were climbing on the slope of one of the hills. Once at the top, we looked at each other smiling, out of breath. Anna leaned on me, holding onto my belt, and pointed toward some invisible spot in the distance.

"That's Baltimore," she said. "If you come back, I'll take you there. You'll like it, since a country like yours must be full of ports. I love the ports."

I returned to New York by train. When I got to Grand Central Station it was after ten at night. I was tempted to get on the ferry and head for Staten Island. I resisted. It was Monday and too late, not regular visiting hours for the Stanleys, anyway. I looked for a telephone booth, couldn't find an empty one, and besides, there were three or four people in line for each one. Well, it was better that way. To seem anxious wouldn't make me look good. The most sensible thing to do would be to arrive in Staten Island unannounced the next day.

That Tuesday was a black one for me. During my absence the editor had decided to do a special issue of the journal, taking advantage of the influx of students who had enrolled for the summer. From minute to minute I wanted to pick up the phone, but the editor kept me hopping, and anyway, I was still in the mood to go to Staten Island without calling first.

I finished around seven, absolutely worn out. The trip on the subway, where I had to stand up, (since there were still some remnants of the rush hour) seemed endless. On the ferry I leaned on the rail and looked out over Manhattan with weariness. A gray drizzle started falling, which drove me to look for a bar where I could get a drink; the whole atmosphere was heavy with warm humidity; I felt sticky, and on top of all that, the beer I had just gulped down was making me perspire heavily. A ferocious headache, something like a migraine, was throbbing at my temples.

At the traffic circle, I hailed a taxi. I lit a cigarette and noticed that my hands were trembling. How could this be, that Damelza could make me feel this way? Here I was, as nervous as a schoolboy about to take an exam, with his mind a complete blank.

When I got out of the taxi, the last rays of the afternoon were washing over Staten Island, interrupted only by a few clouds that were bringing on more quickly the darkness of approaching night. There was only one light on in the house, which was coming from the Professor's study. He opened the door, having heard my footsteps on the walk. He signalled me to come in, with the cordiality that was so characteristic of him, but there was a certain unusual vagueness to his manner, even in his walk.

"Sit down, Alex," he said, motioning me to the sofa across from his reading chair, near which stood a little table with an open book and an empty glass on it. "Let me fix you a bourbon, I'm nearly finished with mine. Oh, I'll fix two, even though I've got two in me already—was it two? I don't know, but anyway, I'll bring the cubes and the bottle; we might need it."

He was back in a moment. "Go ahead, boy, pour yourself one and one for me too; thank you, three cubes for me and three fingers of water, that's right."

He leaned back and sat gazing at me with a curious look in his eyes.

"And so," he said. "I hear you've been away from our little New York."

"Yes, sir, I just got back from Washington yesterday," I said.

"And how did you like that district?"

"I liked it a lot. I got to see some sections of Maryland; my aunt and uncle were very attentive. And how have you and Mrs. Stanley been?"

He leaned forward then and looked straight into my eyes for a moment. Suddenly he asked, "Can I possibly believe that you don't know?"

"Know what, sir?"

He refilled the glasses, and seeing his face in the light, I noticed for the first time how very old he looked.

"Well, it's like this, son, Damelza isn't here, and she isn't coming back. I thought you, at least, would know."

"No, I didn't, sir."

Although I was in the half-light, since the lamp cast its glow over the other side of the room, Professor Stanley must have noticed the effect his words had had on me.

"Well, since nobody else knew anything about it either, except for Dan Corso, since it was he that she ran off with . . . they're living together now in Los Angeles."

"You don't know how sorry I am, sir."

"You're wrong about that, son, I do know," he added. "I know you were in love with her, I know all about that."

"I think I'd better leave, sir."

"Come on, man; don't be in such a hurry. Look, I've been reading, I was when you came—one of the first novels by Somerset Maugham. What a formidable writer he is! You know the intellectuals of his generation didn't appreciate him; they called him frivolous. Sartre and Huxley, and so on, until he was calling himself the best of the second class writers . . . it's true that in his day, the world was lacerated, between two wars, and all that, but listen, he never stopped telling and telling stories, as men will always do, as they've done since the beginning when they sat around the fire in the backs of the caves just for that, to tell stories . . . do you understand?"

Of course I understood. What I didn't understand was what his ramblings were trying to lead to. Under the circumstances, the whole thing seemed, at the very least, dreadful to me, ominous, and my instinct told me to get away from there. I wanted to leave as soon as possible.

"Pour me another drink, will you, Alex? It's very likely that we won't be seeing each other again, at least, not for a long time, you think so? But listen, given the circumstances, you and I are more or less in the same boat, wouldn't you say, but . . . you have an advantage over me, I'm old already, and look . . . yes, you remember when I told you what a great thing it was for a writer to have nostalgia?"

"I remember, sir,"

"Good, that's right, and don't forget it, and maybe when a few years have passed, a lot of years maybe, ten or twenty, you'll feel a powerful nostalgia that calls you, and you'll sit down and write . . . who knows, a story . . . you have a lot of time ahead of you."

It was very late when I left the Stanleys' house.

Poli Délano

was born in Madrid in 1936. As a professor of North American literature at the University of Chile, he began writing short stories and has now published over eight books in this genre, earning for himself a reputation in this specialized field. He has been awarded the Premio Municipal, as well as many other literary prizes of equal merit.

BUT LIFE

THROUGH the half-open window she can hear the strains of music from the organ grinder who sometimes stops to play on the street corner outside her bedroom. There is something very special in the melody today, something sweet and sad, with the deep rich flavor of childhood about it, something that one longs to grasp, to clarify, to hold onto, but can't.

There was too much distance, there was time, and aside from all that, there was fate. There had also been an organ grinder in the town where she'd lived as a child, and he would stop in front of her house by the river with its deep smell of the docks and of tar from the tugboats and fishing craft that plowed through it. He with his little music box grinding out songs, with the little red and blue paper balls that bounced in the air on elastic strings and after a while would burst, showering sawdust everywhere. Children would come pouring out of all the houses by the river at the sound of the first bars of music from the organ grinder. There would be Alicia and René and all the kids from down the block, gathering to stare round-eyed at the wrinkled, sun-browned little man in the huge overcoat that reached almost to his ankles, and they'd watch him turn the handle that magically cranked out songs. When he was finished, he would throw the box over his shoulder, tighten its thick leather straps and shuffle away to the next corner. In the distance they'd see him getting farther away and stopping in front of another row of wooden river houses, and they'd hear the faint music mingling with the river breeze.

What would her mother be doing now in that old house? She wanted to go there, to run down those streets of her childhood, to plunge into the mysteries of the dirty river, to walk along the cobblestones under the rain, to stop in front of that gate and hear it creak on its hinges as she opened it, to cross the cool patio with its cracked paint and chipped mortar, and to go in where the old woman was ironing, throw her arms around her and cry for the lost years. But life, life . . .

The music stops and she hears the shouts of the children; in her imagination she can see the old man and his barefoot horde going off down the street and with him goes something very, very intimate. Now, though, her head is clouded with memory.

She gets up from the bed and goes to the closet. She takes out a little wooden trunk with a shiny lock on it. She opens it and spreads some of its contents out over the coverlet, daydreaming. Here was the photograph of all of them. On the left, her father with his thick moustache, his face tender and severe; he's wearing that striped tie he always wore to mass on Sundays, the same one that went with the blue suit he'd worn that Christmas when he'd waited up for her in the dining room and it was so late she'd tried to slip in without being seen. Two o'clock in the morning. And Julio had left her at the door. What a time! What a night to remember!

"Raquel!" She felt hot and flustered; then a chill went through her. Nothing was going to happen, of course, but . . . what she had done . . . She closed her eyes trying to blot out the memory of Julio and the party and transport herself back here to her own house, and when she opened them, there was her father, taking a watch out of his pocket. He pressed a button to open it, snapped it shut again with a rasping, metallic click and then tossed it onto the table.

"Papa?"

"Come here."

Hesitantly, she took a couple of steps forward. In her father's eyes, she could see that he knew everything.

"Give me a kiss."

"I don't want to, Papa."

"Give me a kiss! You've been drinking."

"No, no, just a couple of glasses of punch at the party. I'm not a child, Papa."

"Have you been with that man? With Julio?"

"Yes, with Julio!"

"Don't be a fool, girl. I've told you over and over I don't want you going out with older men!"

"But he's serious about me, Papa."

"Sure, serious, they're all serious. Look at your cousin Gabey, look what happened to her. She'll be a mother soon, is that what you want to happen to you?"

"No, Papa. Julio wants to *marry* me."

"You won't marry someone who isn't right for you and *young* enough for you besides! And that's that!"

"I love him . . ."

"You won't marry!"

There beside her father is Joaquin, slim, smiling, not married yet, twenty-three or twenty-four. He looks uncomfortable in a suit and tie. He'd look so much better in that brown leather jacket and beret he always wears when he drives his truck. His hands are resting on his mother's shoulders; she's sitting on the long bench, a wise smile on her face, arm-in-arm with each of her daughters—María Eugenia on one side and she, Raquel, on the other, standing in front of her father. 'Sis, I never wanted it this way, I never knew . . .' And she, Raquel, in all the youthful grace of her eighteen years, with a marvelous air of self-assurance of superiority, winking coquettishly at the photographer, a dark young man with black cuffs, on the other side of the camera lens.

There's the group. There they all are, in the living room, that afternoon of that silver anniversary.

And here is a ring, a gold-plated ring. She presses it in her hand now. Inside on the bright surface, she reads: Julio Alvarez P. and the date. She remembers: They were walking toward the station. It was spring. He swore he'd leave everything for her, his house, his relatives, to take her away with him. Her father has given the final refusal. There was nothing else to be done. They would flee to Santiago, the capital, get a special license, make a happy life for themselves. Julio was leading her, and his hand was warm and tender on her arm. His maturity, his forty years, gave her a feeling of infinite security. She loved him even more for all that. What did the twenty years' difference in their ages matter? And the unwanted advice of her relatives and the counsels of her sister María Eugenia, the entreaties of Fernando, Maria's young and dashing knight in shining armor. But Raquel was sure. Nothing was greater than love. It had been her dream, since she was very small, to be passionately in love with someone who could love her, and she'd always believed that someday her dreams would materialize in the form of someone mature, affectionate, tender, and strong . . . Julio. They had left the station now and were near the embassy. Only a few loose ends to tie up. They lay down on the grass in the park and kissed like a pair of teenagers. She would go with him, do whatever he said, follow him wherever he would take her. Julio

269

took out an envelope of black velvet and showed her the two rings. He slipped one of them on her finger and said they'd be married in Santiago, in a few days.

Now she puts the ring on and looks down at her hand, then takes it off and places it on top of the photograph. One by one she starts taking souvenirs out of the trunk, her treasures, her life. Before she knows it, she's crying. She'd wanted it so badly, so very badly . . . A red-orange scarf with the imprint of a kiss on it and the faint odor of perfume that still lingers after all these years. They'd registered in the Hotel El Angelito, on Santo Domingo Street. The place was small and dark, but she'd found it cozy. She didn't mind, really. In a few days, as soon as Julio could get the papers arranged, they would be married and would start looking for a house. They went for a walk downtown. She couldn't find a handkerchief in her purse. Julio took her arm and pulled her into a boutique. A young blonde woman with a lot of make-up on came to wait on them. "A handkerchief for the lady," Julio said, and she showed them a stack of about a hundred. Julio picked one, a bright red-orange one. It was so pretty, Raquel didn't want to use it. Back in the room, where he couldn't see, she pressed her lips against it, leaving a dark red lipstick mark. Then she took a bottle of perfume, poured some of it into it and put the handkerchief away. Now the mark and the fragrance are still there. Five years—how much she'd wanted it! But life . . .

She starts going through the trunk again—trinkets, souvenirs, little presents, all the small tokens of love. Here was the lovely key ring carved in bone that a student had given her. She couldn't even remember his name; she'd only met him once—that one time and never again— better never to have met him, better not to think about it, just seeing the key ring made her cry. What good were tears; they didn't help you. To keep on going, she should be cold, like Julio, but she wasn't. A little key ring—and it was after that that Julio disappeared. Where would he have gone? And why, when he'd loved her so much? He'd loved her so much . . . Be coldblooded, be hard, to survive . . . She throws everything back into the trunk which holds her whole life, slams it shut and shoves it under the bed. She lies back down again. The sound of the organ grinder and the shouts of the children have faded away. A dog is barking somewhere, and the sound of footsteps echoes on the sidewalk. The afternoon is over. She picks up a pack of cigarettes from the nightstand and smokes, thinking. What has it all come to? Will thinking about it solve some problem? She's alone in Santiago, a strange city in an apathetic world. A young woman alone, with nothing going for her except youth and inexperience. Go back home? No! Think, think. But to live you have to eat, not think. So why does she keep thinking and thinking? What does she think will come of all this thinking of what it all comes to?

The two-hundred-pound figure of Doña Marta appears at the door. With a 'whissst!' to wake Raquel out of her daydream, she says, "Raquel, Raquel honey, there's a client in the salon. You've been sleeping all afternoon. Don't sleep so much, it's not good to do that."

"Coming right away, Señora Marta."

She turns on the light, smooths out her skirt, and slowly combs her long thick hair at the mirror. She puts on a little lipstick. She goes out and heads for the salon. A man gets up from the sofa.

"Good evening," he says.

"Good evening. Would you like a drink?"

"Sure, I'll have one."

Doña Marta puts on a record and some high-tempoed tropical sounds emerge from it. Then, her feet shuffling languidly across the tiles, she disappears. The man turns on a table lamp and turns out the overhead light. "There. That's better," he says.

Sure, thinks Raquel honey, sure that's better, much better. Who could he be? He's not old, dresses fairly well. Maybe he's a clerk in some office. Couldn't have much money; the cuffs of his pants are a bit frayed. He's not wearing a ring, but that doesn't mean he's not married. Could this be the one? All these years she'd kept hoping, waiting. There had to be good men, sensitive and loving. There had to be men like that student who'd given her the carved key ring. Could this be the one? And if it wasn't, should she give up hoping? Should she spend her whole life sleeping in the daytime while the sun was shining and the birds were singing? No, it was much better to wake with the day. In the day, her mother would be ironing and her brother Joaquín would be driving his truck. In the day was the *whole* world, the world where men showed their true faces.

Doña Marta comes in with the drinks. She leaves. Always the same. Every time, it was always the same.

"Have some."

"Thank you."

"Cheers."

"Cheers."

"Let's dance."

The man presses her to him, his left hand caressing her breast, sliding his right hand down over her buttocks. As they dance, he opens her legs with his. He starts kissing her on the ear without saying anything. The record finishes and they sit back down on the sofa. He says, "Ready to go?" They walk down the hall to the bedroom. Again it seems to Raquel—to Raquel honey—that she can hear the organ grinder. It's her imagination. Again she can see her house by the river with its smell of the docks and of tar from the tugboats and fishing craft. The stern, affectionate gaze of her father. "You won't marry!" The gate and the cool patio, the room where her mother is ironing. The man takes off his jacket. The cobblestone streets are cool under the rain. The man has taken off the tie and is unbuttoning his shirt. She never thought, never dreamed that this feeling of dread and shame would return. It's been five years; what is there to dread? What's there to be ashamed of? It's not her fault; but something isn't right about all this, she knows that. The man is flexing his arms. "Okay, baby," he says.

"Excuse me a minute," says Raquel, Raquel honey. (The man is undressed and in the bed now.) She leaves the bedroom. Thinking . . . always thinking. But life . . . she thinks, but life. But life is out there somewhere, far away from here. Raquel breathes deeply, opening the double doors and stepping out into the night air. Raquel, Raquel honey, life is out there, far away somewhere. She smiles and looks up the street at the slanting rooftops that line the avenue. Her heart is beating rapidly, too rapidly. She can't resist the impulse to run, down toward the corner, far from here, after the organ grinder.

Marta Blanco

is a journalist, novelist, and short story writer. Born in 1938 in Vina del Mar, she studied at Santiago College and earned first prize in a short story competition sponsored by the journal, *Paula*. Later she became co-director of the same journal. Since 1983 she has been Executive Director for Channel 11 television station for the University of Chile, where she is also a professor. Her major works include *La Generación de las Hojas,* a novel, and *Todo es Mentira,* a collection of stories.

SWEET COMPANION

CHILDREN don't die, Gladys told herself that day. Anyway, things like that didn't happen to her—no one had ever died in her arms. But she could hear the sounds—the measured tread of the competent nurse on the second floor as she paced methodically and efficiently about her duties, oblivious to the real world. Get out! Out of my world! Gladys' mind screamed at her. But what was the point? It would not be appropriate to send her packing just yet—this was not the time to think of being rid of that dreadful white uniform and those obsequious soft-soled white shoes, the immaculately starched cap.

Something horrible was going to happen today—she'd known it from the time she'd first opened her eyes and seen the dense fog hovering in the horizon. She'd heard the neighbor's dog barking on the terrace, seen the laughing children skipping off to school with their school bags and lunch boxes, heard Juan downstairs in the shower and the maids chatting in the kitchen. A day like any other. But death was there, hanging from the walls of this house built just for them, fanatically cared for over the years, painted and polished, its spacious picture windows looking out over the valley and down at all of Santiago, a city wrapped in intangibility and misery.

My little boy. Gladys had an overwhelming desire to scream, or break down and cry. But she was beyond all that now.

That autumn morning, Gladys was beginning to comprehend the full meaning of pain, that there were no words for what was growing in her bowels like a huge poisonous spider; it was nothing like what she'd felt at the death of a grandfather who for so many years had seemed to have no other destiny than to die. She remembered him, fixed in the parchmented limitations of a perfect old age, his stiff white hands with their rough blotches and bulging veins, twisted and blue-nailed, hands made to clutch a cane, to point a finger, to unwrap a caramel, hands molded for the express purpose of folding one over the other, waiting, always waiting. . . .

But a little boy. No. The pain was too full to be bound within these walls, within the rigid ritual of acts and gestures that this house held— the years of examinations, the trips abroad, the piled up hopes of exploring new cures, the self-assured certainty of a recovery, then the boy back in his room with his toys and games, the boy getting weaker, sadder, the boy bedridden, more tests, the bed, the useless toys, the shots he'd had to get used to because only the shots would diminish the pain, relieve the suffering, take away the fear. Now, here she stood, as if nothing were happening, while above her, agony slept, calm and submissive, but growing, sucking him up, taking him farther and farther away from everything he loved and needed, from all his little boy work and little boy play.

The flowering trees were in bloom. Gladys could not, would not go up to that bedroom. It had become unrecognizable as the same room the two of them had arranged together. One by one the favorite things had disappeared to make way for necessary evils—the first to go was the fancy electric train set—it had to move out so there'd be room for the big new bed with its ominous wrist-straps and ankle-straps. Next went the beautiful hobby horse with the real mane, to be replaced by the oxygen tent, and so on. It might as well be an official hospital room now, she thought bitterly; the only difference was that it was here in her house in Lo Curro.

In her less-than-thirty years, Gladys Valdés had acquired a husband, a huge house, five blue-eyed children, and her own car. Two maids, a gardener, and five thousand square yards of lovely gardens completed her perfect world of utter happiness.

None of it mattered now—not the oriental rugs, the copper trinkets, her grandfather's silver, the lovely antique iron gate from the old country chapel on the estate (she'd managed to rescue it when the former tenants had made off with it and to convince Manquileco the caretaker to fetch it back for her), nor the art gallery that had been her pride and joy with famous paintings of Santo Domingo del Molina and the Herrara Guevara statue, even some ugly French paintings (faithful copies of the works of the masters) that her great-grandfather had brought back from his one and only tour of Europe.

It's your fault! screamed all the trinkets and the cobalt collection and the paintings. Your fault for not knowing that sometimes a child can die, your fault for not making him someone special, for not taking him out to the field where the wild flowers grow and the honey bees make their hives. She could have shown him cocoons and the transformation of the caterpillars into beautiful butterflies. They could have talked about the clouds, picked up baby birds fallen from their nests, put them in shoe boxes, and fed them with vitamin droppers; she could have given him a pet rabbit to keep in a cage.

But why couldn't I have known from the beginning? Why wasn't I told, why, why, why? And now it's too late and he's dying, the poor little thing, and all I can do is stand here planning it, getting everything ready for it, always getting things ready for tomorrow, for that grand and perfect afterwards, organizing time that can't be organized, filling up the days with children and rules and dos and don'ts and straightening everything that's crooked and putting things back in their places and cleaning and polishing and embroidering and mending torn overalls and discipline and ritual and always saying no to everything.

Improvisation had never had a place in the life of Gladys Valdés. Until today, with death forcing an impromptu appearance in the little room on the second floor; until today, with the improvisation of a journey through the medicine bottles, the smells, the wrist-straps and the ankle-straps, the bloody cotton wads and the soiled sheets; until today, the only surprises had been a cake or a picnic, or maybe the news of the death of the laundry woman's son.

"How is he?" Juan was meticulously clean shaven.

"Today," she said, and realized she was not going to cry.

"Don't talk foolishness. We don't know anything."

"It's today," she repeated.

"I'm going to call my mother."

"Don't let her bring that rosary into the room," Gladys heard herself say. "And I won't have her crying all over him. He's afraid, do you understand?" It was then that Gladys realized it would not be absolute improvisation. She would help him die the best death possible, to leave his body and slip softly into final submission. She would confront the whole family, the grandparents, the great-grandparents (did a great-grandfather have the right to watch a great-grandson die?), so

Gonzalito wouldn't have to hear the moanings of the mourners in the privacy of his bedroom.

"I don't understand," Juan said.

"He's *afraid*." A tear escaped her—one solitary tear that she caught with her tongue before it could roll all the way down to her chin.

"What time's the doctor coming?"

The doctor. Gladys recalled that cold austere personage, saw him leaning against the mantel telling anecdotes about his race horses or his deer hunting in the islands of the southern lakes. Now she realized that he was going to be taking on the role of the main actor in the death of her child—to be the concrete mark of familiarity that would sooner than necessary be turning the whole thing into a ceremony of mourning and litany with the house filling with uncles and aunts, cousins and godfathers, and relatives of every sort. Juan's only defense was to put it all in order, disguise it, smear it over with tears and rites, with people coming and going. Sheltered by the living, he was already forgetting the reality of the death.

"There is no defense," said Gladys, more to herself than to him.

"I have to call my mother. And I'm not going to the office."

"Look, the sun's coming out. That's nice."

"It makes no difference to me," he muttered. "I can't take any more of this."

But suddenly it was necessary for Gonzalito to die. It was absolutely essential that he die in his pretty little room on the second floor, so they could all go on with their normal lives and so that the house could take on its normal smells, its normal routine and acquire a sense of stability once again.

Gladys went up to the room.

"He's calm, Mrs. Valdés. Very calm." The nurse went to the window, raised it to let in the fresh air and quietly left to go down to breakfast.

Gladys looked down at her son. She took the pale thin hand in hers, and Gonzalo opened his eyes.

"Hi."

"Hi. I feel good. I want some hot chocolate."

"Okay. I'll fix you a great big cup of nice hot chocolate."

"Right now."

The nurse came in and Gladys went down to the kitchen.

"I've been up to see him, Juan. He feels good. I'm taking him a cup of chocolate."

"Chocolate! Are you crazy? He can't have anything heavy!"

"Don't worry about it, Juan. He's happy."

Coming back with the steaming cup, she could hear Juan's voice in the bedroom, and she took the stairs two at a time.

"How's the little man? Ready to play ball? You don't want chocolate, Gonzalo, it'll make you sick! Wait till the doctor gets here. You'll never get better that way!"

"I want some chocolate."

"But you'll never get better if you don't . . . listen to me, Gonzalito, for God's sake!"

Gladys came in with the cup and a smile. The father went out, slamming the door behind him.

"Look, how delicious."

"Mama, I want to sit up."

She set the cup on the nightstand, fluffed up the pillows, and straightened the comforter. As she took his thin body in her arms, she felt something shrink inside her. He sat up and took a few spoonfuls of chocolate.

"Mama, I don't want anymore." Tiny drops of sweat were breaking out around his lips.

"It's okay, baby."

The boy closed his eyes. His body was trembling with the effort to breathe. She turned on the oxygen and pressed the mask over his face. "Breathe, Gonzalo, breathe, see, now you're better. . . ."

"Tell me a story, Mama."

"Once there was a beautiful princess who lived in a white palace. . . ." As she told the story her eyes never left his face, and she prayed that sleep would come to him and take him off to those magic places where deep within the hearts of all children, a story is always waiting.

At last he drifted off. Then the grandmother came in.

"My baby!" she sobbed, throwing herself on the bed.

"Sara, please, not now."

"My poor grandson . . . my treasure . . . angel, don't leave us!"

"Sara, please leave." Taking her mother-in-law's arm, she conducted her to the door. "We mustn't wake him up now, understand? He gets scared. He's so young. . . ."

"He's dying, my poor baby's dying!"

"Sara, go down to Juan. He needs you."

"But I want to pray for him!"

"Downstairs, Sara, downstairs."

"But . . . why?"

"Because."

She was no longer surprised at her new-found strength. All those nights of watching over her son had hardened something in her, something that was growing and affirming itself. She understood that she was the mother of Gonzalo above all the cares of the world and that this death belonged to her because she was now filling up with ancient tradition and secret wisdom—just as now within her were cohabitating strong unknown beings, old Hebrew mothers, stout Roman matrons who understood death in all its power and austerity.

My God. To think of the grandmother and how she'd buried her husband amid weeping and wailing and convulsions and prayers and everyone hugging and kissing all over the place. Gladys remembered her father-in-law's death, remembered the human smell that clung to the pillows and the brass bed, the three days of agony and crying, of visitors going in and coming out with the smell of death on them which was none other than the smell of all of them.

A pigeon landed on the balcony. The boy opened his eyes. She was smiling, so he smiled.

"Look," she said. "Look what a pretty pigeon just landed."

"He sure is pretty," Gonzalo murmured in a thin voice. "He sure is pretty, Mama."

Gladys shook out the white coverlet and straightened it. She wanted everything smooth and perfect, immaculate. She went to the dresser and arranged the medicine bottles, the syringes, the wash basin. She placed the photo of the family in front.

"Mama, I want to play monopoly."

"Okay, but I'm gonna win."

"No you're not. I'm gonna win."

She spread the game out over the coverlet, shuffled the game cards, and got out all the little pieces, chose two and threw the dice.

"My turn, Mama."

"Yes, but no cheating."

He threw the dice and moved. "I don't want to play anymore. I'm tired."

"Sleep if you want to. We'll finish the game later."

"And the other pigeon, Mama? The little one? Where's he?"

"He died," she said quickly.

"Why, Mama?"

"Because, Gonzalito. Just because."

She sat down on the soft white bed and stroked his forehead, his eyelids, his hair.

"Hey, Mama, am I ever gonna get better?"

"Of course, love. Why wouldn't you?"

"I don't know, it's just that I can't remember school."

He closed his eyes. She could feel again that certainty that sometimes came and went, the certainty that Gonzalo knew and that he was searching for confirmation, for help, that he was done with being lied to because he was preparing himself for the final test, as he'd been doing all these years, to pass the course.

Our Father who art in Heaven. Hallowed be thy name. Thy kingdom come, thy will be done on Earth as it is in heaven . . . Father in Heaven, help us . . . help me to help him through this . . . Don't pity us, but help us, and don't leave us . . . let him sleep so he won't suffer.

"Mama! Mommy, I feel bad!"

Gladys knew then that she was going to have to endure again the horror of the hemorrhaging, that she would have to endure her child's fear of seeing his own blood gushing over the white coverlet, that she and the nurse would have to hold him down while the vomiting and the convulsions went on, through the tears and the panic, until the bleeding stopped and the drugs should put him to sleep.

"Mama!" The blood spurted out of his mouth in a thick red stream and spread as he cried in her arms and the nurse prepared the injection and stuck the needle into his arm marked with needle holes. The bleeding lessened little by little and the child fell back against the pillows, his eyes dilated with fear.

"It's over now, love, it's over, don't be scared, it's all over. . . ." She was leaning over, cradling him to her, letting the stain soak into her blouse and down to her chest until she was almost stuck to him. The boy closed his eyes again. Together, she and the nurse washed him, changed him, and changed the sheets. When they were finished, Gonzalo felt for her hand and lay staring at her, hungrily, longingly.

"Mama. Pretty Mommy. I love you," he said and fell asleep.

"I'm going to call the doctor," the nurse said, putting away her blood pressure apparatus.

The boy opened his eyes again and looked at his mother without smiling. But she smiled. She was going to keep smiling, as long as he could still see her, always, oh God, always.

"Hi, Mama."

"Hi, love."

"You're pretty."

"You're handsome."

"I'm sleepy but . . . don't leave. . . ."

"No, honey, I'm not leaving."

He took her hand and squeezed it and laid it across him. "Don't leave, Mama. Not until I. . . ."

Gladys knew for certain then that her son knew what she knew and that the test was growing in both of them, and they would be together in it.

"Don't worry, darling. I will never leave."

His father came into the room. "How is he?"

"He's fine," she said.

"Go get something to eat, Gladys. I'll watch him."

"No."

"I'll be here with him."

"We'll both stay."

Juan looked down at the pallid figure of his son. He stood by his wife for a while, but the silence was more than he could bear. Finally he tiptoed out of the room.

The doctor came in. Gladys was sitting rigidly beside the bed.

"Yes," she was saying to the nurse. Then the nurse noticed too the change in his breathing. "Do you hear?" she whispered.

"No," he said. He moved closer to Gladys and put a hand on the boy's head.

"He isn't suffering."

"I know," she said. Nothing was going to happen to her son now. He was free.

Carlos Pastén

was born in Antofagasta, Chile. He left Chile in 1973 where he had been a professor of Spanish-American literature at the University of Chile. He now lives in Toronto where he directs the cultural programs for Spanish speaking people. His stories and articles have been published in Chile, Winnipeg, and Toronto.

LAW OF ESCAPE

It was five o'clock in the afternoon, and they had already brought us some cold cuts when we heard the doors of the cell open. The twelve of us socialist prisoners were still in the jail. The communists and the revolutionary leftists had been banished to far-off regions, and very few had been released. We looked worriedly and searchingly into one another's eyes, counting one another, supporting one another. We were expecting to hear the voice of the devil, but instead, we barely made out the silhouettes of a police officer and a prison petty officer. The latter spoke up violently:

"These prisoners are to form a line in the passageway: Carlos Gallegos, Breno Cuevas, Vicente Cepeda, Julio Brewe, and Adriano Naveas . . . Adriano Naveas?" he ended up on a surprised note, looking at the police lieutenant who apparently wasn't Alex Cantín.

"Yes, Adriano Naveas, Corporal."

"Excuse me, Lieutenant, it's not possible."

"What do you mean, it's not possible! Don't you know we have orders?"

"But Naveas is in solitary confinement by order of a civil court, Lieutenant,—we have to have a court order to get him."

"What court order? Everybody here carries out military orders!" Both men had retreated a little to the dark side of the passageway. As they argued, our comrades busied themselves with picking up jackets and blankets, taking advantage of the discussion to gain a few more minutes. Dr. Cepeda came up to me and slipped me a folded piece of paper.

"See if you can give this paper to your wife so that she can give it to mine. As you know, I haven't had a permit to receive visitors. I haven't been authorized, and it's quite possible we'll be there for a long time."

Assenting, I took the paper and put it carefully inside the sock on my right foot.

It was routine to take the prisoners from the jail to the police station and there put them through intense torture to interrogate them. We saw them when they left and we tried to encourage them with comforting looks and gestures. We heard the heavy bolts of the door echoing as they locked it after them. We had been shut up for more than a month in this common cell where the light was never turned off. We would sleep fully dressed on the cement floor and sometimes cover ourselves with a blanket. Some of our friends who had gone had left behind things that all of us used: sweaters, towels, and the two mattresses that we took turns using. This afternoon passed more quietly than most. Some of us played chess, others tried to read the Bible, the only book permitted. The police station was adjacent to the jail and our cell, located right beside the police station yard. Because of this, we could hear some of what was happening there on the other side.

We fell asleep early. It was unlikely the police would take out another prisoner for torturing.

I think I woke up seconds before I heard a cry and shots from a machine gun. I heard the shots go off two or three meters from where I was lying. I rolled off the mattress into a corner of the cell. I was shivering. I tried to check my body, I saw that everybody had jumped up, but then we stood motionless. I heard the sound of pebbles falling down on the tin roof like drops of rain. Questioning cries, doors slamming, insults, and people running back and forth followed our astonishment. It hadn't happened inside our cell. There was as much activity and noise on the other side of the wall as there was stillness and silence where we were.

"It happened on the other side, in the police station," someone said. Everybody understood that.

"Have they killed Vicho and Carlitos?"

"What time is it?"

"Two minutes past four."

"That means it must have happened at about four o'clock in the morning." We stayed quiet. Suddenly we heard an order that surprised us.

"Take away these rebels and rinse the floor to clean off the blood." We heard murmurs, grumbling, footsteps, moans.

"Is this son of a bitch ever heavy!"

We were all pale. Then old Casimiro got up and went to the bathroom; we heard him vomiting at the same time as we heard the sound of brooms sweeping the cement.

It was impossible to go back to sleep. Thousands of questions came to our minds, but it was useless to ask them all. We smoked in silence. On the other side, all was quiet at last.

It was five o'clock.

Six o'clock and still nobody could sleep. The doubt was anguish. Seven o'clock and we started to hear the usual movement in the cells. One guard and several delinquents who always fixed breakfast, among them the man we called "the devil," passed through the passageway to the yard.

"Hey, Corporal, what happened last night?"

"I don't know, really; we don't know what happened in the police station—we're just as curious as you are."

Eight o'clock in the morning. Suddenly we could hear a radio. Music. The sound came clearly. It was not the first time; on several occasions we had heard music from this same radio.

Eight-thirty and then we heard the news. "News update report. At four o'clock this morning, as four political prisoners attempted to escape from jail after overpowering the guard posted outside the cells, they were shot and killed instantly by other guards. The four prisoners were Vicente Cepeda, thirty-one years old, physician from the Cobrechuqui Hospital, Breno Cuevas, forty years old, Health Inspector at the Tocopilla Hospital; Carlos Gallegos, thirty years old, teacher at elementary school Number 13 of Tocopilla; and Julio Brewe, thirty-two years old, teacher at the Tocopilla High School."

A shudder ran down my backbone, and I thought immediately of Nano Naveas.

"We repeat, at four o'clock this morning, as four political prisoners attempted to escape from. . . ."

"It's strange they've let us all stay together in one cell, don't you think?"

"But I think it's better for us this way."

"Yes, of course, at least we can talk about whatever we want."

"In fact, we could escape together."

"What?"

Everyone looked at Brewe, surprised.

"Okay, you're the leader of our party, but don't be stupid."

"But they won't kill us, I'm sure of that."

"If they were going to kill us, they would have done it already."

"No, no, no. I think the party's just starting, and we won't be dancing for a while yet."

"Quiet! How many times have they interrogated us already? You, for instance, they've tortured you four or five times. They haven't gotten much information and the cops know they won't get anything more from us. They beat on us just for revenge. If they had decided to kill us, they wouldn't have punished us as much as they have."

"Then why do you think they brought us back to the police station?"

"Hey, why don't we change the subject. I'm more nervous than a parrot on a high wire and now you start talking about all this stuff."

The night came on, a dreadful and expected night, a night filled with uncertainty. Any slight noise made them think the policemen had come back to torture them.

"Have they been busy interrogating the people from the pampas?"

"Or are they just keeping us for tomorrow? Well, anyway, they don't seem to be in a hurry."

Around four o'clock in the morning someone knocked on the door of cell number five.

"Hey, Corporal, come here a minute, will you?"

After a moment the iron door to the passageway to the cells opened.

"Corporal, Carlitos Gallegos is sick and he needs to go to the bathroom."

One of the cells, in fact the last one in the row, had a toilet.

The policeman, wearing a heavy cloak, opened the door with some difficulty as he carried a heavy machine gun in one hand.

Gallegos went out into the passageway, bent over as if suffering from a terrible stomach pain, followed by Cepeda.

"Hey, you . . . stay inside!"

But Cepeda quickly took the machine gun from the surprised policeman. Brewe had already gagged him from behind; meanwhile, Cepeda knocked him out with one blow. They dragged him quickly into the cell.

"I hope to God the iron door is open."

"There must be another policeman on guard out there."

Silently they slipped out, close to the wall. The door was half open, not locked. The other cop was smoking in the center of the small yard.

"We've got to surprise him too, quick!"

Shoving the door open, the four men burst out, but this policeman was ready with his machine gun. He squeezed the trigger and the bodies were thrown into the air, rebounding off the cement wall. A few moments after the surprise, all was confusion. The lights of the building were turned on and a large number of policemen and officers came running with their guns firing.

"It's strange they've let us all stay together in one cell, don't you think?"

"But I think it's better for us this way."

"Yeah, sure, at least we can talk about whatever we want."

"It would be terrible to be all alone in a cell waiting for them to come to torture or kill you."

"And what do you think we're doing, having a holiday or something?"

"Of course not, I mean being totally alone in a cell going crazy."

"I hope to God they don't hit me so much on the nose this time."

"Is it really broken?"

"Of course it is; do you think I'm faking?"

"No, I don't mean that . . . Did you ask for another doctor?"

"What fascist doctor wants to come and look at a colleague who's an accused terrorist? He would be scared to death. Anyway, I've fixed the dislocated bone myself; it still hurts, but not as much as it did."

Seated on the wooden platform, they covered themselves with the blanket they had brought from the jail. Evening had turned into night.

"Who do you think they'll take out for torturing this time?"

"Let's make a bet."

They looked at each other and stayed quiet for a while.

"Hey, Corporal, can we have a smoke?"

"Did you hear; he said okay."

"Corporal, we don't have any cigarettes; how about giving us a few."

"You bastards've got your nerve!"

Nevertheless, a hand threw a couple of cigarettes and matches through the little window of the cell.

"Incredible, they're still good!"

"I hope this isn't like the condemned man's last wish."

"Why don't you shut up."

Instinctively, they huddled together to light their cigarettes, which they passed around. They breathed in deeply and slowly exhaled the blue smoke into the darkness of the room.

"What time is it?"

Conversation became difficult, almost impossible. They sat in silence, wrapped up in their own thoughts.

"The hardest part is the uncertainty. I think I wouldn't care if they sentenced me to ten or twenty years in jail, but the important thing is to know what's going to happen, once and for all."

"And to think I voted for Alessandri instead of Allende and now here I am accused of being a terrorist, a revolutionary."

"Then why did you become a socialist?"

"After all, at some point in your life you can be on the right side, can't you? And even though they've beat the hell out of me, I'm not sorry. I just wish everything hadn't happened so fast; we never had time to realize how important the whole process was."

"It's true, we've been so superficial, so inconsistent, so irresponsible."

"I disagree. We just never had the chance to live out our great experience; we were busy with other things, like the birth of our children, loving, living. It wasn't until now that we decided to fight for the great cause, and we didn't know how to solve the practical problems."

They sat quietly for a long period of time again. Then they heard footsteps approaching. Quickly, they stood up and folded the blankets, thinking the cops were coming for them. The door opened with the same terrifying sound.

"Come out, one by one."

"All of us?"

The moment they were out of the cell, several policemen took hold of them; one of them tied blindfolds around their heads, another tied their hands behind their backs, but what surprised them was that the other cops put gags in their mouths. With each policeman holding an arm, they were led out with some difficulty. This time, the way was longer than on other occasions, and they even got out to the street. The group came to a small truck that was waiting for them at the rear of the police station. The cops shoved the four prisoners into the truck. The vehicle started with a squealing of tires. Half an hour, forty-five minutes travelling over a dirt road. The bumps and turns thwarted their efforts to get free of the ropes and prevented their groans from being heard. When the drive was over, the cops pulled the prisoners out. One of them fell down, but the policemen stood him back up. They looked like small shadows among the enormous rocks. The sound of the crashing waves muffled all other sounds. A policeman with a cigarette in his mouth tried to strike a match. Suddenly, the flash of machine gun fire erupted, throwing bodies to the ground like listless rag dolls. Lieutenant Alex Cantin gave the machine gun to his assistant.

"Finish them off with a pistol shot to the head."

"Right away, Lieutenant."

It was even more difficult to light the cigarette, for the wind from the sea snuffed out the flame.

"News, update report. At four o'clock this morning as four political prisoners attempted. . . ." I stretched out my hand to my right foot and took out the folded paper.

Dear Angelica,

Please try to find out as soon as possible about going to Argentina. Tickets, passport, schedules. Take the money out of the bank and keep it. I believe I'll be free very soon. Try to get permission from the warden to see me here in the jail. Give Angelita a little kiss.

I love you,
Vicente

As my eyes filled with tears, I folded the paper and put it back in the sock on my right foot.

Juan Carlos García

was born in Santiago in 1944. He studied at the Valdivia Normal School, at the Southern University of Chile, and at Queen's University in Kingston, Ontario. He is currently completing his Ph.D. in literature at the University of Toronto. He has published short stories in Chile, Canada, and other countries.

THE EARTH-EATER

HE would wander up and down the main road that led to town un-til he found a good place. He would take a stick, like a tree branch or a piece of old wood to use for a shovel, and then he'd start digging, piling up dirt on both sides until he was sitting between two small mounds, with a gaping hole in front of him about the size of a dried up water hole.

Passing him on our way to school, we had our suspicions, but we kept our secret, not wanting to be robbed of the pleasure of returning each day to find the piles of dirt gone from around him. We had to be sure so we stayed out of school one day- we wanted to find out if he really was using the stick as a spoon and gobbling up that dirt by the mouthfuls as we suspected.

All morning long, we kept watch—the hours passed as he just sat there like a silent statue of stone. When afternoon came on us, we were tired and ready to give up and go home, when suddenly the stick in his hand, heaped with dirt, began to move slowly toward his mouth. We watched spellbound as he shoved a pile of it in and began chewing and smacking. Ignorant of or oblivious to our presence, he chewed for a long time with great gusto; then came the second mouthful, then the third and the fourth, each time eating faster and faster, until by about the ninth or tenth mouthful, he had broken all the records for any eat-ing contests we had ever seen. When we left our hiding-place, there were no more little mounds of dirt near him, and the pit in front of him had grown by a few square feet. But boys being what they are, we kept our secret and he continued eating up the earth, night after night in the little town.

One afternoon, the police came by the school. They came to ask questions; that was clear enough. But we were mum. Some said he was selling land to the Peruvians; others denied it. Some said he was selling water; others argued that it wasn't so, that he'd made a deal with Argentina, that he had a pact with the Devil, and so on. So the police went back to their headquarters and spent the rest of the winter asking among themselves whatever questions they could.

The mayor and council members took it before the town council at the first spring meeting. By this time, we had already stopped hiding out to observe him, for now our uncles and grandfathers would take us down the road to watch. It was the most astonishing spectacle in the town's history. (The only other incident like it was that of a Columbian girl who had once lived in Macondo.)

The mayor and the town council agreed that they should put out a flyer with some sort of warning, but worded carefully so as not to alarm the populace, also giving assurance and suggesting a number of ways to maintain order and keep the peace. But none of this was necessary, since the whole town was dizzy with order and stunned to speechlessness at the sight before their eyes. Finally, the mayor decided that all he needed to do was to put a restriction on the boundaries from which the people could observe, and to prohibit any public disturbances at the observatorial site.

Very soon, the County Collector got the idea of closing off the area by erecting portable walls with peepholes in them so people could watch for a small fee. As the Earth-eater kept gobbling up earth, the walls had to be moved, and new ones built, with more peepholes, because his fame had spread to the neighboring towns.

Anyway, with the money earned from the spectators who came to watch the Earth-eater, all sorts of new buildings went up, hospitals for gentlemen, schools for gentlemen, hotels for gentlemen and their young ladies, even a telephone system for men and women. In a word: the town flourished. This cycle kept up until one day the main street was eaten through and the town was divided. The mayor on the other side built a new school on our side, and pretty soon a hospital and some new hotels, until finally, we didn't know exactly when or how it came about, but we realized it was time to elect our own mayor and our own beloved town council.

So the years went by, and with all the prosperity brought by the perpetual activities of the Earth-eater, interest began to slough off. Indifference set in. People stopped coming from other towns to see him eat dirt, and the people of our own town stopped coming, neither from our side nor the other side. The profits began to fall until they hit zero. And since they had to keep moving walls around, the two mayors stopped assuming the responsibility until neither one would do it;

so finally, at the new spring session, it was decided that they would dispense with the walls altogether and leave his activities free and unrestricted.

Apparently, this decision provoked in the Earth-eater a boundless increase in appetite. After that he started gulping down dirt night and day; more roads were found to be cut through and deep ruts began to appear all through the city. Naturally, we began to feel some alarm, which grew to fear, then to insurmountable terror as the adult population stopped thinking about offices, schools, factories, and hospitals in their preoccupation with the Earth-eater. Now, besides dirt, he was chomping up plants, trees, little animals, and had already glommed some of the humbler houses in the humbler sections of town.

Now the townspeople tried to retract their previous mandate of un-restriction; they wanted to re-erect walls around him, repair the broken roads, elect one mayor, and impose some kind of personal tax or fine on the Earth-eater himself.

But all their efforts failed, and many had to leave town, for a great number of us had already lost our homes, aunts, uncles, and dear mothers, all swallowed up by the Earth-eater with no pangs of conscience whatsoever.

Years have passed since the day when we boys first saw him there on the road to school. I heard something about him on the news the other day, for since that time, he has gone from town to town, gobbling up flower beds, street lights, automobiles, bridges; demolishing schools; devouring factories; and swallowing people like peanuts. Those of us who had first seen him eating dirt had never imagined the capabilities of the overwhelming power of his gluttony. And this, I think, is the reason we are still alive today.

THE FLOOD

ONE morning, near the end of autumn, Gregorio Lipincoy woke up to the sound of water dripping onto the bed. Half-asleep, he figured that the rain, which usually filtered through the cracks of the old apartment where he lived, had finally found its way into his bedroom. Since the drip had already formed a wet circle that was beginning to smell rank, and since the spot was already up to his left elbow, Gregorio Lipincoy had no choice but to clear his thoughts and try to think of a way to fix it so he could go back to sleep. His first idea was to move the bed a few inches the other way; at least the drip would not be getting the bed any wetter. But then, he thought, if he let it keep dripping on the floor, the sound would get louder and louder and would eventually become an endless drumbeat in his head. To prevent this, he decided to move the bed and place a cloth under the drip to absorb the water and muffle the sound. Since this seemed to be the best thing to do, he stretched, yawned long and loud, and started to get up to execute his plan.

Touching his feet to the floor, Gregorio Lipincoy was surprised to find that he was stepping into water. For the first time, he looked around and discovered that the whole bedroom was submerged. Naturally, he thought, it's a flood. As he stood up in the water, an odd idea struck him, like a feeling of a bad omen, but he quickly dismissed it.

Thinking more clearly now, he grabbed some clothes to put on and stumbled out into the hall, still dressing. The water was up to his ankles.

The hallway that led up to his door was full of water. It was as if the rain had been falling for hours and hours inside the house, with no roof or walls to stop it; also, it was as if nobody had noticed it, for Gregorio could hear no familiar noises, not the usual clatter of the cleaning woman, or the familiar racket of the rowdy students and working girls that lived in the old apartment house with him.

From the door of his bedroom, he then noticed that the other bedroom doors were all ajar, and the main door to the street was wide open. Suddenly Gregorio was struck by the strangeness of it all. He felt an urgent desire to run outside and find an explanation for it. Lifting first one foot, then the other, he went along making a slow, splashing noise that seemed to hover, stagnating in the air behind him in the hall. With a determined effort, he advanced toward the outside door, looking into the other rooms as he passed to see the effects of the flood and to assure himself that there was nobody there.

When he reached the doorway, he stood and stared. It occurred to him that he might just be dreaming. The street, like the house, was full of water, and in front of him were passing dozens of people: women holding up their skirts, men with their pants rolled up, children with teddy bears under their arms, and all of the people formed lines that moved from east to west, west to east in a slow, endless, liquid procession.

Confounded, he shouted, "What's happening?"

"The water is rising!" was the shouted reply from those passing near him.

It took him a few seconds to realize it, but suddenly he noticed that it was not raining. Still, if it wasn't raining, why was the water getting deeper and deeper? For it was now up to his knees.

He felt a dull, sickening shiver go through him. He told himself that since the rain had stopped, all this would pass in a few hours. He thought of his friend Julian. He would go to Julian's house and tell him about the flood, and Julian wouldn't believe it. They would come back and have a look at it, and they'd have a good time laughing about it. He was comforted by this thought; just think of all the good laughs they would have at the funny things he was seeing now: old ladies in their long underwear, telling whoever would listen about how they were awakened so suddenly; fathers carrying radios and disassembled cribs; teenage girls with their make-up cases, their skirts held up above their knees; civil employees ridiculously dressed in suits and ties, but with no shoes on; women who'd been caught in the kitchen, carrying their pots and pans; college students, deliriously happy; and all these arranged in orderly lines walking—or rather sloshing—in step, with no apparent purpose or direction.

Deciding that the best thing to do was to find Julian as quickly as possible and show him all these strange sights, Gregorio joined the people. He wondered how far the flood waters went. "How far back does it go?" he asked someone. "To Japan," was the response. When the words sank into his mind, he smiled. He remembered how his grandfather had always told him, "A good sense of humor is the best antidote for troubled times."

He turned a corner and started walking south. He looked as far ahead as he could, trying to make out Julian's house, and he noticed that not only did the waters extend that far, so did the lines of people. They were moving from north to south, south to north. Julian's house was half-covered. It's the whole section of town, he thought.

Then, he began to get very angry and excited at so much water. He supposed that the main lines must have burst. They must have exploded; there was too much water here for just a rain. He stopped in front of Julian's house and called to him. The people around him complained for him to keep moving, but he continued calling. Those behind him pressed against him, until he fell to his knees, pushed by the yelling crowd. Several furious and desperate people cursed him and shouted angrily for him to get up and walk. Someone helped him to his feet. "Walk, son," he heard in his ear. He walked. He decided that he would have to play along, so as not to have any more trouble. To amuse himself, he thought about how funny it would be to find Julian walking in the opposite direction, with his pants rolled up, trying to explain how and why all this flood had started.

The water was now up to his testicles. Since there was nothing but water as far as he could see, he began to think it necessary to know how far he should walk, and to get out of this damned inconvenient situation. Determined now to get an accurate response, he shouted, "How far is the flood?"

"All through the town," they shouted back. Exasperated by the vague answer, he told them in a sarcastic tone, "They say it goes to Japan."

"Well, to Japan, then," they answered.

Now, for the first time since it had started, Gregorio felt like a fool. Everyone else knew something he didn't, he decided. Yeah, that was it; he was just ignorant of what was going on, how long the town had been flooded, how far it extended, and all the details. He felt infinitely stupid and ridiculous. Unless he found Julian, his fate might well be that of a hapless victim. A desperate need to get to dry ground washed over his soul, and his splashing became more intense, more frenzied and frequent, along with the splashing in his stomach.

The line in which Gregorio moved had reached the main street of the town. From there he could see the train station and he noticed an incongruous mass of objects floating around the people. There were apples, tomatoes, carrots, books, and flowers. There were suitcases, desks, dining tables, and chairs, all rocking gently upon the waves of Main Avenue. So the waters have reached the shops along the underpass, he thought. So the waters have covered the train station. And he felt that a light had been snuffed out inside him somewhere. He imagined floating automobiles and train cars, with people arranging their lives on them until the waters should go down. Half-walking, half-floating, Gregorio headed toward the train station and went in. Hundreds of men, women, and children were standing in the sooty water on the railway platform, looking to the north at water as far as the eye could see. He saw train cars standing still, with the people on them looking as if they were waiting for the trains to float them away to dry land. The people there were motionless. He noticed that the only place where the people were motionless was on the train platform. The water was up to his chest now. He saw a little child with water flowing into its mouth, trying desperately to climb higher into its father's arms.

A feeling of sadness and terror swept over Gregorio as he realized that he was not able to help the child. He felt as if the flood were demoralizing him somehow, as if it were ravaging some moral principle of his that Julian was always talking about. Gregorio thought that if Julian were here, he would certainly not be feeling this paralyzing, suffocating terror that he now felt as the waters rose to his shoulders. When he felt his feet leave the floor, his head rocking on the surface among the other floating bodies, Gregorio thought how awful it was not to have been able, at least, to find Julian so he could tell him where the flood had come from. Suddenly, for the very first time, Gregorio Lipincoy realized that he was afraid of dying.

EPILOGUE

The flood had begun at dawn, according to most reports, although some said that days or weeks or months before, the fields had appeared soggy, and there were reports of ruined crops, wet apartments, and streets with unexplainable pools of water. Since at that time Gregorio couldn't have known about all these unfortunate occurrences, he turned out to be one of those who disappeared in the flood. Don't ask me how he disappeared. A lot of them disappeared. Many of us tried to help: we caught bodies and tied them to lamp posts or we sustained survivors and helped them join our lines. People began to find dry places and moved to streets in neighborhoods where friends or relatives lived. Long columns of people formed, having no apparent destination. Still, many realized that the columns were made and led by those experienced with water: scuba divers, professional water-football and hockey players, city water company workers, and managers of the hydro-electric companies.

After the flood waters began to go away, we could see many dead bodies ripped open by vultures, some without eyes and noses, wearing ugly grins. The dead were scattered all over the countryside. Many were found and identified. Not Gregorio Lipincoy. We looked for him, and we continue to look for him, but up until now, our efforts have been in vain.

Carlos Iturra

was born in Santiago in April, 1956. He is studying law, philosophy, and diplomacy. He has participated in many fiction writing workshops with José Donoso and Enrique La Fourcade. For four years, he has been one of the literary editors and critics for the newspaper *El Mercurio*. Primarily a fiction writer, his work has appeared in anthologies and literary journals. In 1983, he won first prize in the short story writing contest of the magazine *Paula* for his story "El Apocalipsis según Santiago."

A DROP OF IMMORTALITY

THEY saw each other for the first time—and I know of no second—in the parlor of the regal mansion of Victoria Campo, where a group of wealthy, well-known, and prestigious men had gathered to chat. Actually, to say "saw each other" is erroneous—or at least ironic—*he* saw Borges, who at the time was distractedly watching the vast brilliance of the sun setting over the ocean. Alone on the cool terrace of creamy marble, they talked of Sterne, of literature, of travel books—laughingly imagining one written by Kant. But somehow or another, they digressed into the topic of the immortality of the soul. Perhaps what led to the discussion was their advanced years and the view of the fading day. . . . The professor was rambling, not without sadness, about the unequaled writings of Plato, of the African Father, and of Monsieur Comte. Borges then recalled with equal passion Macedonio Fernández and the extensive debates he'd had on him; thus convinced, he believed himself to possess now the tenuous certainty of an everlasting destiny. "I doubt," he affirmed, "that death can be anything more than a mere physical act, and I believe that I, like Rosas, like Shakespeare, like yourself, like our friend Fray Bentos, am something more. Something much, much more."

Abeliuk, longing for even a shadow of the security that he saw in Borges, fell into a tirade of argument in which he denied all hope of this and in which he expressed his odious conviction that dust and the worm conquer all, all. With fatalism, with something of the desperation of those who don't aspire so much to convince each other as to convince themselves of their convictions, the two men debated the topic until the evening had plunged them into utter darkness.

Days later, alone in his apartment in Palermo before a pale and fading sunlight, the Professor began to reflect again upon the conversation of that evening—especially upon the things he'd left unsaid or had said in haste—to his disgust. *That* was what stuck most in his mind about the incident, for though he was not so well-versed on the subject, he had anguished within for so many years about these fears, had carried the burden so long, that he felt himself qualified to speak on it.

Every bit as common as the vastness of the sea, the air, the declining of the day, and the declining of life, is the commonness of man's yearning to live forever. And just as those who believe in eternal life are smugly content in their knowledge, so those who doubt, like Lafcadio Abeliuk, are condemned either to despair or to the faint prospect of immortality through works or through children, knowing that works and children are also destined for the "cold silence of the stars," but not being able to aspire to transcendencies less ephemeral, they grasp onto the meager consolation that these hopes humbly bring.

So Professor Abeliuk felt these longings to endure, as was natural for a septuagenarian—profound, painful, and in the end if he but knew it, futile. And even more painful because those things which most afflict the mind and soul are those which can never pass the lips, painful for the humiliation that comes from simply carrying them, futile because at his age he was already hopelessly declining. It was already too late to have the children he'd never had and create the works he'd never created. With all his brilliance of learning and his recognized erudition, the Professor—obstinate in his faith in knowledge and wisdom, with the sterility of all time that was now his—waited for death to incorporate him into absolute nothing.

So he thought looking into the last flames of sunlight on the horizon, I, Lafcadio Abeliuk Toll, Professor of Classical Languages, Professor of Ancient History and Hebrew Philosophy, who can appreciate literature in more than seven languages; expound on Whitehead, Porphyrius, Jansenism and the dogmas of Jesus; who never could quite believe in God; who have never written a novel, but have countless monographs collecting dust on recondite shelves; now have to die without ever having grazed the surface of the luminous meaning of life. Soon to take my leave of a life without meaning that seems to have no justification other than the birth in myself of this desire to be eternal. My renowned learning has not contributed toward the creation of a single poem, not one worthy story, nor has it helped me to resolve any of the essential mysteries of life, much as I would fantasize that it has. With all my knowledge and intelligence, it just comes to this: What . . . use . . . has . . . it . . . been . . . to . . . me . . . ?

I should mention here that these obsessions did not continually perplex him so. They would recur from time to time to break into his daily routine of perusals in the various heterogeneous volumes, and his note-taking in various homogeneous notebooks. Something like the conversation with Borges.

A second conversation took place with that well-known author about two months after the first, this time by telephone. Borges had just come back from a long trip; it was morning when Abeliuk heard the phone ring. They greeted one another cordially, and after some small talk, discreetly, quietly, in his own way, Borges brought the conversation around to what it was he'd called about. "The reason I called you, Professor, is that I've written a story in which I mention your name and I wonder if you would give me permission to print it. My secretary can come by your house this afternoon and leave you a copy. The scene is about an imaginary Turkish sect that prospered in the eighth century, and you and I get into a debate about it. The story is called 'The Conventicle of Fire.'"

Abeliuk responded that to confer such an honor on him it was not necessary to ask permission, that naturally it would be okay, and thank you so very much.

That afternoon, he read the story and read it again and re-read it. It was one of Borges' best, and would hold its own against such previous successes as "The Circular Ruins" or "The Fork in the Garden Path." The same tense language, the same exactitude of abysmal and terrible ideologies that had made him famous; all were found in this story. And because it pertained to him personally, he read it all the more avidly.

The third conversation took place that night and was of no importance. He called Borges and congratulated him. Later, lying in bed, his customary insomnia was even more heightened by the very thought that his name would be part of a story that was about to become known, undoubtedly, on a grand scale, futuristically with considerable translations and footnotes.

When Emece published it in a small edition of a thousand copies entitled *The Sword of Thor,* the critics were unanimous in their praise. They celebrated the author's having surpassed even his former works and praised his wonderfully thematic innovations, predicting renown for that volume.

It would be difficult to describe the state of mind felt by Abeliuk during those days, principally because no one tried to find out, and we can only suppose. Maybe he vacillated between happy embarrassment, crumbling pride, and despair. Maybe he thought of the walled city of literature infinitely more well-known to him than to those who lived within it, into which he could never pass, but must always spend his life just outside of. Maybe he saw himself stealthily trying to sneak into it, a stowaway, placing on one of its buildings a plaque with his name on it. Maybe through his mind passed visions of yellow deserts with clouds of sand growing more and more distant to the unreachable confines of longing, of silent subterranean streams, or maybe his visions were so indescribably vague that they were not even images that could be transcribed into words.

The fourth conversation took place on a dark rainy night in autumn. It's a fact that this hour of the day produces ineffable feelings of nostalgia and of paradises lost that can never be repossessed, also that the autumn itself brings upon the soul a feeling of rare sadness. Wrapped in a dim light, the Professor calmly dialed Borges' number and waited. His words were, more or less, the following:

"Yes, I believe I can better explain my reasons later. But for now, it's just not possible, since I doubt that I could define them clearly even to myself. But certainly, there are strong motives that you will understand more when you know them. At this moment, suffice it to say that I implore you urgently to take it permanently out, and not to let it appear in another published edition."

After having exchanged farewells and hearing the click of the line on the other end, Abeliuk, receiver still in hand, added, "To a vicarious continuity, to the ecstatic pleasure of a drop of immortality, to an everlasting borrowed memory, I prefer—ultimately, silently, eternally, terribly, and simply—the forgotten."

INDEX

POETRY

FICTION